Grenada
Revolution in Reverse

James Ferguson

To my parents

First published in Great Britain by the Latin America Bureau (Research and Action) Ltd, 1 Amwell Street, London EC1R 1UL

Copyright © James Ferguson

British Library Cataloguing in Publication Data
Ferguson, James
  Grenada: Revolution in Reverse

British Library Cataloguing in Publication Data
Ferguson, James
    Grenada : Revolution in reverse
    1. Grenada. Political events, history
    I. Title II. Latin America Bureau
    972.9845

ISBN 0 906156 48 3 pbk
ISBN 0 906156 49 1 hbk

Written by James Ferguson
Edited by Duncan Green

Cover photo by Chick Harrity/*US News & World Report*
Cover design by Andy Dark/Art Depot

Typeset, printed and bound by Russell Press, Nottingham NG7 4ET
Distribution in USA by Monthly Review Press, 122 West 27th Street, New York, NY 10001

Printed on recycled paper

Contents

Grenada

Principal roads

.... Parish boundaries

0 1 2 3 Miles

0 1 2 3 4 Kilometres

PETIT MARTINIQUE

Hillsborough

CARRIACOU

CARIBBEAN SEA

Levera Bay

Duquesne Bay

Sauteurs

Grenada Bay

Victoria

ST PATRICK

St Patrick R.

Lake Antoine

ST MARK

Gouyave

La Poterie

Grand Roy

ST JOHN

PEARLS AIRPORT

Telescope

Great River Bay

Grenville

Grand Etang
Lake

MARQUIS I.

ST GEORGE

St Andrew's Bay

ST ANDREW

Grand Mal Bay

Gt Bacolet Bay

ST DAVID

ST GEORGE'S

La Tante R.

Crochu Harbour

St David's

Grand Anse Bay

Westerhall

Morne Rouge Bay

INTERNATIONAL
AIRPORT

Frequente

Westerhall Bay

Point Salines

Egmont Harbour

Lance aux Epines

HOG I.

CALIVIGNY I.

CARIBBEAN SEA

Grenada in Brief

Statistics

Area	344 sq kms (including Carriacou and Petit Martinique 48 sq kms)
Population	103,400 (1987)
Growth	2.4% (1984-7)
Migration	2.0% (2,000 per year)
Capital	St George's (9,000)

The People

Origins	Afro-West Indian 91%; East Indian and Syrian-Lebanese 6%; White 3%
Language	English; local patois
Religion	Roman Catholic 60%; Anglican 20%; Methodist 3%; Seventh Day Adventist 3%; other denominations 14%

The Economy

GDP (1988)	US$139.1 million
GDP per capita	US$1,346
GDP real growth	1984-7 4.9% 1987 6.0% 1988 5.3%
Exports	1988 US$32.5 million
Imports	1988 US$92.1 million
Trade Deficit	1987 US$56.7 million 1988 US$59.6 million
Principal exports (1988)	Nutmeg and mace 44%; bananas 14.5%; cocoa 9.8%; clothing; rum
Major trading partners (exports)	UK 30-35%; CARICOM 20-25% West Germany 8-10%; US; Canada; Netherlands
Major trading partners (imports)	UK 25-30%; CARICOM 25-30%; Hong Kong; Japan; US; Finland

Tourist arrivals
(1988)
Stopover   61,795
Cruise ship   135,980

External Debt   1987 US$45.9 million
                            1988 US$48.7 million
Internal Debt   1987 US$34.9 million
                            1988 US$35.9 million
Debt servicing as
% of export earnings   20.3%
Debt as % of GDP   41.7%
Unemployment   34.5%

The Society

Literacy   85%
Life expectancy   63 years
Infant mortality   15 per 1,000
Doctors per head
of population   1 per 4,400
Currency   Eastern Caribbean Dollar (EC$)
                            EC$2.70=US$1 (1989)

Sources: Caribbean Development Bank, *Annual Report* 1987 and 1988;
Caribbean Tourism Research Centre; *Caribbean Insight;* Economist Intelligence
Unit; *Latin America and Caribbean Review* 1988 and 1989.

Acronyms and Abbreviations

AAWU	Agricultural and Allied Workers Union
AGWU	Agricultural and General Workers Union
AIFLD	American Institute for Free Labor Development
CAIC	Caribbean Association for Industry and Commerce
CANA	Caribbean News Agency
CARICOM	Caribbean Community and Common Market
CBI	Caribbean Basin Initiative
CCAA	Caribbean/Central American Action
CCC	Caribbean Conference of Churches
CDB	Caribbean Development Bank
CDLP	Christian Democrat Labour Party
CDU	Caribbean Democratic Union
CEP	Continuing Education Programme
CIA	Central Intelligence Agency
CIDA	Canadian International Development Association
CPE	Centre for Popular Education
CPF	Caribbean Peacekeeping Force
EC	European Community
ECIPS	Eastern Caribbean Investment Promotion Service
EDF	European Development Fund
ESF	Economic Support Fund
FAO	Food and Agricultural Organisation (United Nations)
FTZ	Free Trade Zone
GDM	Grenada Democratic Movement
GDP	Gross Domestic Product
GFC	Grenada Farms Corporation
GISCO	Grenada International Service Corporation
GMMIWU	Grenada Manual Maritime and Intellectual Workers Union
GMMWU	Grenada Manual and Mental Workers Union
GNP	Grenada National Party
GULP	Grenada United Labour Party
GUT	Grenada Union of Teachers
HIAMP	High Impact Agricultural Marketing and Production Program
IDB	Inter-American Development Bank
IDC	Industrial Development Corporation
IFAD	International Fund for Agricultural Development
IMF	International Monetary Fund

INSTEP	In-Service Teacher Education Programme
MBPM	Maurice Bishop Patriotic Movement
MNIB	Marketing and National Import Board
NACDA	National Cooperative Development Agency
NDC	National Democratic Congress
NED	National Endowment for Democracy
NDP	National Democratic Party
NDF	National Development Foundation
NIS	National Insurance Scheme
NISTEP	National In-Service Teacher Education Programme
NJM	New Jewel Movement
NNP	New National Party
NTS	National Transport Service
OAS	Organisation of American States
OECS	Organisation of Eastern Caribbean States
OPIC	Overseas Private Investment Corporation
PFU	Productive Farmers Union
PRA	People's Revolutionary Army
PRG	People's Revolutionary Government
PTS	Public Transport Service
PSYOPS	Psychological Operations (US Army)
PWU	Public Workers Union
RMC	Revolutionary Military Council
RSS	Regional Security System
SSU	Special Service Unit
SWWU	Seamen and Waterfront Workers Union
TAWU	Technical and Allied Workers Union
TNP	The National Party
TUC	Trade Union Council
USAID	United States Agency for International Development
VAT	Value Added Tax

Foreword:
An Empty Victory, An
Uncertain Future

The United States of America can boast of two military victories since the end of World War II: the invasion of Panama in December 1989 and the 'intervention' in Grenada in October 1983. The Grenada invasion involved 6,000 US troops against some 600 Cuban construction workers and 250 local militia. Even with these odds, victory was unexpectedly difficult to secure.

It would be even harder to claim any other sort of victory in Grenada. The official success story, of course, is one of rolling back communism in the Caribbean and installing democracy and freedom. Or, with a slightly different emphasis, of reversing a revolutionary, non-capitalist development strategy in a West Indian mini-state with guns, dollars and privatisation. That questionable success, however, has left a bitter taste in the 'spice island'. Today, more than six years after acquiring the dubious distinction as the first Commonwealth country to be invaded by the US, Grenada hobbles to an uncertain future, economically and politically.

In the wake of Ronald Reagan's 'Urgent Fury' invasion, former Secretary of State George Shultz tellingly described the island as 'a lovely piece of real estate'. Today, it looks more like a sad caricature of the free-market, private sector-led paradise that it was meant to become. Nor is it a shining example of the virtues of Westminster-style parliamentary democracy.

On 13 March 1990 Grenada held its third general election since independence from Britain in 1974. The results confirmed three inescapable facts. First, that the electorate is reluctant to risk its future with another radical political programme at a moment of dramatic and far-reaching change throughout the world. Second, that for all their success in dismantling the economic infrastructure and social welfare projects of the People's Revolutionary Government (PRG), the US and the Grenadian political establishment have yet to find a credible alternative to the revolutionary legacy. And third, that this political vacuum came close to producing a return of the terror, corruption and buffoonery associated with the politics of 'Gairyism'.

It was the rule of Eric Gairy, marked by electoral fraud and thuggery, that back in March 1979 had led to the first revolutionary seizure of power in the English-speaking Caribbean. In a region first dominated by London and since by Washington, the government of the charismatic Maurice Bishop and his New Jewel Movement (NJM) colleagues turned centuries of colonial rule on its head. For 4½ years, Bishop and the PRG struggled to pull Grenada out of its historic dependency and underdevelopment, looking for imaginative solutions to entrenched problems. That period of excitement and great potential was to end in the nightmare of sectarian strife and political executions, followed by foreign military invasion.

Subsequent developments have not produced a government capable of taking up the challenges posed by the PRG. Instead, under US tutelage, Grenada's professional politicians have made various alliances and coalitions, only to split and regroup in new combinations. The New National Party (NNP), formed in August 1984, was little more than a vehicle to prevent Eric Gairy from returning to power. It won elections in December 1984 on a strong anti-Gairy vote and with open US encouragement. Half way through its term of office, however, the government, led by Herbert Blaize, was already in pieces. It was this NNP administration which in a gesture of self-contempt named President Reagan a 'national hero' of Grenada. Its policy was simply to squeeze as much aid and investment out of the US as possible. But within two years of the invasion, the image of Grenada as a showcase of democracy and free-market growth had become a mirage. The long-awaited flood of dollars never appeared.

With the death of Herbert Blaize in December 1989 and the final demise of the NNP government, Grenada faced its second post-invasion election. This time, five parties wrestled in an atmosphere of traditional West Indian bacchanal politics. But by now the frustrations, alienation, disappointments and confusion felt by many Grenadians had combined to produce a low turn out and an inconclusive result.

What emerged was a new coalition of forces, made up of even stranger bedfellows than those who formed Blaize's cabinet in 1984. With the help of a defector from Gairy's camp and two survivors from the party which Blaize had founded just before his death, Nicholas Brathwaite's National Democratic Congress (NDC) was able to put together a government with a 10-5 majority. This arrangement followed a traumatic week of deals and manoeuvring during which the prospect of fresh elections loomed large.

The current NDC government is seen by many as the result of an uneasy truce, characterised to a large extent by political self-interest. Few believe that it has the philosophy or the support to carry out the the unpopular fiscal and economic measures needed to steer Grenada out of the serious problems it faces. Nor does it seem to be a government that will have the capacity to restore to Grenadians some of the dignity and self-respect of which they were robbed by the invasion of their own country.

The tasks facing Grenada's rulers in the 1990s are immense. They must look to alleviate the depressing problems of a mini-state, where half of households are still without access to electricity and running water, where 40 per cent of young people are unemployed and where many live apprehensively in a climate of social tension and rising crime.

Grenada: Revolution in Reverse is, in the circumstances, a most timely publication. In analysing the policies of the post-invasion governments, it provides a valuable sequel to the Latin America Bureau's earlier book, Grenada: Whose Freedom? which explored the rise and fall of the 'revo'. As memories of the US invasion fade, this book traces Washington's subsequent failure to turn Grenada into a model of democracy and economic liberalism. Following developments from the invasion itself to the present disillusionment with the US role, it offers a wealth of hard information and incisive observation. It brings to those interested in the Caribbean a quality of analysis essential for understanding a new phase in US foreign policy and the current predicament of the region.

Rickey Singh
Barbados
April 1990

Introduction
'Urgent Fury'

'A period of self-doubt is over...history will record that one of our turning points came on a small island in the Caribbean where America went to take care of her own and to rescue a neighbouring nation from a growing tyranny.'
Ronald Reagan, 25 October 1984.

'We blew them away.' Vice-Admiral Joseph Metcalf III, 3 November 1983.

On 25 October 1983, the largest military action carried out by the United States since the Vietnam War until the invasion of Panama took place in the tiny Caribbean island of Grenada. Codenamed 'Urgent Fury', the operation actively involved 6,000 US marines and paratroopers, with thousands more in reserve. A further 400 paramilitary personnel from six Caribbean states were indirectly involved, although none took part in the actual fighting. The total cost of the exercise was later estimated by the US Department of Defense at US$75.5 million. Its avowed objective was to invade the island, oust the *de facto* government that had been in power since 19 October and return Grenada to the US sphere of influence after four years of socialist revolution.

The invasion, claimed President Reagan, was conducted with 'surgical precision'. In reality, it was a clumsy display of incompetence, poor intelligence and what military strategists call 'overkill'. Not only did the invading force meet with unexpectedly fierce resistance from a small number of Grenadians, but it also engaged in wholly avoidable conflict with Cuban construction workers at the site of the new airport. In one of the many bombing raids which were intended to destroy specific targets, a psychiatric hospital was apparently mistaken for a military base when a number of Grenadian troops fled into it, and some thirty patients were killed. Much property was destroyed, while high military and civilian casualties were incurred due to inadequate communications, lethal 'friendly fire' and an emphasis on aerial attacks. The operation took three days longer than anticipated; it was only on 28 October that a press statement, intended for publication on the 25th, was released to confirm the success of the invasion.

Mental Hospital Bombing

The most controversial D-Day destruction . . . was that of the 180-bed mental hospital. The attack on the mental hospital was made by an A-7 Corsair light attack aircraft with a 500-pound bomb. The result was devastating. 21 Grenadian patients were killed according to US official estimates — and over 50 according to journalists who first discovered the death and the destruction. One will never know the exact number. The attack on the hospital was undoubtedly unintentional. It was what has nowadays come to be called 'collateral damage'. What is surprising is not that the mistake was made, but the fact of the failure by US officials to acknowledge that Grenadians had died in the attack. Official acknowledgment of attack on the mental hospital came on 31 October, six days after the Grenadians had been buried. The US marines who had been in the vicinity of the hospital for almost a week, it seems, did not report the matter to their superiors (or did they?). Admiral Wesley McDonald . . . said that he first learnt of the attack from the ham radio operators. But he did nothing till a Canadian journalist visited the site and made the bombing and the death and destruction public. The explanations for the attack were then advanced. It was asserted that the hospital was attacked because it did not have a red cross marking on the roof; that the PRA had raised a flag on it; that it was near Fort Frederick (which strictly speaking also did not deserve aerial punishment); and that the lunatics inside had been armed. The failure to find out about the hospital dead was explained by claiming that it was due to the Grenadian custom of 'burying their dead early'.

Source: Vijay Tiwathia, The Grenada War: Anatomy of a Low-Intensity Conflict, p.87.

Like the Falklands war the previous year, the Grenada invasion was an important exercise in official misinformation and media control. Just as the extent of US casualties was underestimated, so the number of Cuban personnel — and their military status — was deliberately

Jim Rudin

US soldier in streets of St George's, 27 October 1983

exaggerated in order to explain the difficulties encountered. Reliable reports suggested that the bodies of Grenadian soldiers were flown back to Havana with the Cuban dead so as to minimise the local death toll and inflate the Cuban casualty figures. Thirteen such corpses were returned to Grenada from Havana in late October and early November. The invading force attempted unsuccessfully to restrict news coverage to selected journalists, and most 'unofficial' reporters were effectively prevented from reaching Grenada until the military action had ended.

The official version of events, however, failed to prevent criticism of the efficiency of the operation and the grounds on which it was based. The three immediate justifications for the invasion — that US citizens, notably students attending an 'offshore' medical school, were in danger, that Grenada's Governor-General had requested assistance, and that the Organisation of Eastern Caribbean States (OECS) was entitled to invite US intervention — have all been subsequently revealed as spurious. Equally dubious was the longer-term rationale for the US action: that Grenada, and the new airport in particular, were intended as a staging post for Cuban and Soviet aggression in the Caribbean and Latin America. Despite statements from the

British-based electronics company, Plessey, that the airport was unsuited and unequipped for anything other than civilian purposes, the US Department of Defense insisted on displaying stockpiles of largely antiquated light weaponry as evidence of a threatening military build-up.

One aspect of the invasion did not have to be invented, however; the fact that the great majority of Grenadians welcomed the arrival of the US troops. The atmosphere of relief was therefore interpreted as a popular endorsement of the military action. If this much was true (even though civilian populations normally have the good sense to welcome invading armies), it was certainly much more questionable to assert that people were also celebrating the demise of the revolution. This, of course, was the image that the US State Department conveyed, but such an image overlooked two central details: that the revolution and its popular support had already collapsed six days earlier with the death of Maurice Bishop and others; and that the US 'rescue mission' was therefore saving Grenada not from revolution, but from a military coup that had already destroyed that revolution.

The reasons for the destruction of the Grenadian revolution have been extensively analysed and debated elsewhere (*see p.15), and there is little to be gained from repeating the arguments that have made up its post-mortem. It is simply worth remembering that the dispute over leadership and ideological direction which split the New Jewel Movement (NJM) culminated in the murder of Prime Minister Maurice Bishop and five of his leading supporters on 19 October 1983 at Fort Rupert, St George's. With this action and the further deaths of an unknown number of civilians at the hands of the army, ended the 4½-year regime of the People's Revolutionary Government (PRG) and began the brief period in power of the Revolutionary Military Council (RMC).

For six days the RMC ruled by decree, attempting to impose a 96-hour total curfew throughout the island. Grenada's overwhelmingly agricultural population was forbidden under pain of death to tend crops or feed animals. Few Grenadians had reserves of food, and shops were closed indefinitely. Many people without inside sanitation were in theory prohibited from leaving their homes. Government radio repeated accusations against Bishop and his supporters, but little was known concerning what had happened at Fort Rupert or how many had died in the massacre. Reports that bodies had been left unburied, burnt or thrown into communal pits caused widespread revulsion which combined with a more general sense of trauma. Arrests and detentions of 'counter-revolutionaries' were common, and although no recorded violent death occurred during the period of curfew, the atmosphere was one of fear and uncertainty.

The arrival of the US troops was therefore greeted with understandable enthusiasm by a significant number of Grenadians, including many who had supported the PRG. For some, the first priority was revenge against the RMC which was held responsible for Bishop's death, and the invasion seemed to offer such retribution. Had the invasion occurred earlier, the popular response would certainly have been different. 'If Bishop had been alive, leading the people', remarked Fidel Castro, 'it would have been very difficult for the United States to orchestrate the political aspects of its intervention.'

Setting an Example

The invasion restored the self-esteem of the Reagan administration, whose foreign policy initiatives were following the general pattern of post-Vietnam failure. After Washington's disastrous involvement in Lebanon and impasse in Central America, Grenada offered the prospect of an easy propaganda coup. As Bob Woodward relates, the invasion became a potent myth for President Reagan and his presidency:

> Grenada grew as a positive symbol in Administration lore. It was routinely invoked as a sign of a new toughness, reaffirming the Monroe Doctrine, big-stick and gunboat diplomacy — anti-Communism — burying once and for all the specter of Iran. The images were those of American students returning from Grenada, kissing US soil as they disembarked from airplanes, or a defiant Prime Minister Charles [of Dominica] at Reagan's side proclaiming the United States the savior of Caribbean democracy.

Undertaken in the name of national security and regional stability, the initial motive of the invasion was, as former Secretary of State Alexander Haig admitted, geo-political. Its function was primarily to demonstrate US military control of the Caribbean region by putting into action the 'Reagan Doctrine' which proposed 'rolling back communism' by military means. But once accomplished, the invasion also opened up a further possibility.

With the military victory won, the opportunity now existed to make an example of the island. Since 1979 Grenada had been viewed by Washington as a Cuban and Soviet satellite. Within the terms of the prevailing East-West conflict, this meant that Grenada was a military threat, but it was also a country which followed an economic and political model unpalatable to the US. According to the Reagan administration, the PRG was moving rapidly towards sweeping state control of the economy and the forced collectivisation of agriculture, stifling individual enterprise in a welter of red tape. Worse, it was allegedly engaged in human rights violations and had established a repressive one-party state. The invasion could therefore be presented to the world as a liberation from communist tyranny and as a warning that socialist development was not a feasible option in the Caribbean.

As well as issuing this warning, the invasion also offered the opportunity to score an important ideological point by proving the superiority of the US-endorsed economic model for development. Washington hoped to discredit the revolutionary period by emphasising its supposed economic failures, and simultaneously to demonstrate the advantages of the US model by turning Grenada into its showcase. The island would become a laboratory for an experiment in development that would replace the non-capitalist approach of the PRG with the free-market capitalism favoured by the US administration.

US policy in the region was at that stage in the Reagan presidency precisely geared towards such crude ideological goals. The function of the so-called Caribbean Basin Initiative (CBI) of 1983, for instance, was to increase US aid and trade with selected countries in an attempt to strengthen links between their governments, local private sectors and US investors. Loyal allies of US regional policy such as Jamaica and the Dominican Republic were rewarded by increased bilateral aid and by valuable preferential access to otherwise protected US markets. Grenada, of course, had been excluded from the benefits of CBI for as long as the PRG had been in power. With the destruction of the revolution, however, the island was seen as a potential model for private sector-led development in a Caribbean micro-state and as a vindication of US regional policy generally.

This tempting possibility had less pleasing financial implications. By cutting Grenada's links with Cuba, the Eastern bloc and various Third World countries, the US cut off much of the financial aid that was channelled into the PRG's development strategy. Having shunned the island's request for assistance for the previous four years, the US now found itself committed to playing the major role in Grenada's economic affairs. Repairing the damage done during the invasion promised to be a costly business, as did the prospect of building an infrastructure that would attract US investors. But the long-term aim lay precisely there, in the belief that private investment would provide the basis for Grenada's transformation from socialism to the free-market model.

This belief did not take long to fade into disappointment. Significant private sector investment has never materialised in Grenada. If the idea of a free market showcase ever existed seriously, it has long since disappeared. Grenada's story since October 1983 is that of Washington's failure to turn the island into a textbook model of free enterprise in the Caribbean.

Revolution and Reaction

In the immediate aftermath of the invasion, most Grenadians supported the US action. Some sections of society, particularly the small business sector, which felt themselves to have suffered during the PRG regime, were enthusiastic, and within several weeks the local Chamber of Commerce had organised a 6,000-strong petition demanding a permanent US military presence in the island. Most Grenadians, however, were more ambivalent, even if hopeful that US aid and investment would bring a new prosperity. While welcoming the end of the RMC, they were concerned not to lose the significant gains made during the four years of the PRG. These gains had affected the lives of the overwhelming majority of people and were almost universally popular. Rooted in the commitment to transfer wealth and power to the traditionally poor and marginalised, the PRG's major social reforms formed the basis of its non-capitalist development programme. Their impact was felt in many key areas:

— housing: the PRG introduced low cost housing for the poor and a system of home improvement grants and loans that benefited an estimated 1,600 families;

— health: free medical and dental treatment was introduced for the first time. In the PRG's 1982-3 budget, 14 per cent of expenditure was devoted to health care, and at least one medical centre was established in each of the island's six parishes during the four years of the 'revo';

— education: the PRG introduced free primary and secondary schooling, offering free uniforms and textbooks to children from poor families. In 1978, three Grenadians were studying abroad on scholarships; in 1983, the number had risen to 330, of whom 50 per cent were educated in Cuba and 50 per cent in Eastern Europe. Education accounted for 22 per cent of the 1982-3 budget;

— employment: the PRG created thousands of jobs in an expanded security force and in infrastructural work. Unemployment dropped from an estimated 49 per cent in 1979 to approximately 14 per cent in 1983, largely due to state schemes

Philip Wolmuth

Trade unionists march to celebrate the third anniversary of the revolution, 13
March 1982

such as the Youth Employment Project which placed some 1,000 young people on training and work experience courses in agriculture and construction;

— women: a separate ministry of women's affairs was formed. It introduced paid maternity leave, pre-school and day centres, and campaigned successfully for the removal of discrimination in pay and conditions. Women benefited particularly from the literacy and adult education campaign organised by the Centre for Popular Education (CPE). The institutional sexual exploitation endemic to the previous regime was effectively eliminated;

— wealth: the government claimed a rise in per capita annual income from US$450 in 1978 to US$870 in 1983. Income tax was abolished for the lowest-earning 30 per cent of the workforce, while prices of essential items were strictly controlled;

— participation: the PRG involved thousands of people in decision-making through mass organisations, trade unions and zonal councils. The 1983 budget was discussed throughout the island by local groups, comments and criticisms being sent directly to the ministry of finance. Bodies such as the National Youth Organisation and the National Women's Organisation had 6,500 and 7,000 members respectively at the peak of their influence.

The Colonial Period

1498   Christopher Columbus sights Grenada during his third voyage

1609   First British attempt to colonise island repulsed by indigenous Carib population

1674   Grenada becomes official French colony after extermination of Caribs

1763   France cedes colony to Britain at Treaty of Paris

1795   Inspired by Haitian slave revolt, 'free coloured' planter Julien Fedon leads unsuccessful 15-month insurrection against British authorities

1838   End of slavery

1857   Cocoa replaces sugar as main crop

1951   Eric Gairy leads general strike

1962	Constitution suspended after British commission finds evidence of corruption by Gairy government
1973	New Jewel Movement formed; mounting protests against Gairy regime
1974	Grenada achieves independence

The legacy of social reform that the PRG left in Grenada was all the more remarkable given the island's history up until the revolution of March 1979. Grenada's evolution from sugar-producing colony to dependent micro-state had followed many of the stages common to most Caribbean territories. The gradual process of colonial withdrawal by the British promised to favour a small dominant class of landowners, merchants and state functionaries who controlled much of the best land, the export-import businesses and statutory agricultural marketing boards as well as the public sector utilities. The vast majority of people were politically and economically marginalised by this elite which was prepared to consolidate its power through an alliance with the colonial authorities or, if need be, through political independence. A middle stratum also existed, comprising urban professionals and larger-scale farmers, but the majority of Grenada's population were rural workers, employed on the estates, engaged in peasant production and small-scale trading, or commonly a combination of these. The shift from sugar as main export crop to newer crops such as bananas, nutmeg and cocoa had done little to affect land distribution in the island; in the 1950s it was estimated that 1.45 per cent of Grenada's farmers (or perhaps some 150 individuals) owned almost 45 per cent of the island's cultivable land. The creation of the 'spice island' had also involved the replacement of slavery by the system of *metayer* or share-cropping, whereby peasants worked on estates in return for rented smallholdings.

Extreme social inequality, colonial neglect and deteriorating conditions generated serious conflict throughout the Caribbean region in the 1930s and 1950s, resulting in increased trade union and political party organisation. The 'slums of the empire' thereby produced a generation of leaders who were to be instrumental in the process of political independence, thus obstructing the anticipated succession of the established colonial elites. In Grenada's case, Eric Gairy, a mercurial and populist trade union leader, rose to power by claiming to represent the island's traditionally marginalised majority. Using his union base to create a political party, Gairy went on to win five out of seven general elections between 1951 (when universal adult suffrage was first introduced) and 1979.

The 'Slums of the Empire'

In 1946 the Slum Clearance and Housing ordinance was enacted, specifically to provide proper houses for persons of the working class, to eradicate slum areas and to repair or demolish insanitary dwellings. By 1949, the Central Planning and Housing Authority (the executive authority established by that ordinance) had built 12 houses, and these were for persons who lost their homes during the 1945 floods . . . By the end of the 1940s, 86% of the houses in Grenada were still wood, wattle and mud; 80% were either one or two-room dwellings with no privacy for adults . . .

The standard of peasant infant care was very low. Between 1935 and 1950, an annual average of 400 children born in the hospital went home fat and healthy only to return in a few months in an advanced state of marasmus due to neglect and improper and insufficient feeding . . .

Many children had nothing to wear except rags or 'shirt-tails' and many were kept away from school due to lack of adequate and proper clothing . . .

The 1938 Commission on Economic Conditions among Wage-earners described the peasant's housing as disgraceful, his clothing as wretched and his body as emaciated by hookworms, venereal disease and tuberculosis. His children were ravaged by yaws and gastro-enteritis. These conditions still prevailed by 1949. In that year the Labour Commissioner reported . . . protein, vitamin B, calcium and Iron deficiencies in the diet of workers and their children.

Source: George Brizan, *Grenada: Island of Conflict,* pp.240-241.

Based on clientelism and thuggery, Gairy's later periods in office were marked by economic mismanagement and repression. A colonial commission of enquiry in 1962 accused the Gairy government of systematic corruption ('squandermania') and political victimisation, and briefly suspended the colony's constitution. Ridiculed for his apparent obsession with flying saucers, Gairy's more serious failings included links with Pinochet's Chile and Duvalier's Haiti. To the British authorities, eager to be rid of their Caribbean colonies, Gairy was scarcely the ideal candidate for leading Grenada to full

Jim Rudin

Eric Gairy's government on Independence Day, 7 February 1974. Gairy is seated fifth from right

independence. Nevertheless. in 1974, amid widescale protest and state-sponsored violence, Gairy cut the island's formal colonial links with Britain.

Revered by many poor Grenadians who remembered him as the militant unionist of the 1950s and the self-appointed spokesman for the black majority, Gairy was anathema to the 'plantocracy' or land-owning elite who resented his crude populism and pilfering of government money. In response to Gairy's Grenada United Labour Party (GULP), the idiosyncratic vehicle for its leader's ambitions, the economic elite set up an opposition Grenada National Party (GNP), founded in 1956. Led by Herbert Blaize, a barrister from the dependent territory of Carriacou, the GNP was an orthodox conservative organisation, devoted to representing the interests of estate owners, the Chamber of Commerce and the urban middle class. It was in office twice (1957-61 and 1962-7), during which time the country stagnated.

The GNP, however, was unable to defend its constituency against Gairy's attack on the plantocracy. Given much more power by the internal self-government granted by Britain in 1967, Gairy introduced a 'land for the landless' programme which amounted to the expropriation of political opponents' estates in the name of agrarian reform. Gairy took over many large agricultural properties between 1968 and 1973 and simultaneously rewarded GULP loyalists by purchasing their farms at inflated prices. In this way, he built up a significant state sector, based on a system of patronage and corruption. He also ensured a solid stratum of rural support by handing out smallholdings to landless estate workers.

Besides victimisation and nepotism, the alternation in power between the GULP and the GNP produced few significant changes in actual policy, despite the fact that the parties claimed to represent the rural majority and the urban elite respectively. Overt clientelism was common to both, as was uncritical support for US policy in the region. This combination of corruption and conservatism was the background against which the radicalism of the New Jewel Movement (NJM) flourished. A history of dubious electoral practice also accounted for the NJM's open distaste for the discredited 'Westminster model' of parliamentary democracy, even if, for tactical reasons, the NJM entered an unsuccessful electoral coalition with the GNP in 1976. The extent of popular support for the insurrection which ousted Gairy in March 1979 showed that most Grenadians were eager for the social transformation that the NJM, as principal political force within the PRG, promised. Gairyism and the conservatism of the GNP seemed to belong to the past.

Return of the Old Order

The destruction of the PRG and the resulting overthrow of the RMC created a power vacuum in Grenada that the US was determined to fill. Soon after the invasion, old faces reappeared. Following four years of exile in the US, Eric Gairy returned to the island and resurrected the GULP, while Herbert Blaize, who had spent the revolutionary period in obscurity in Carriacou, revived the GNP. To many observers, the impression was one of *déjà vu* and dismay that the seemingly discredited Gairy and Blaize could once again lay claim to political power.

Their return, however, was not merely symptomatic of the post-invasion power vacuum, but also of the resilience of their support bases during the revolutionary period. The remnants of the plantocracy and the small business sector, the sponsors of the GNP, had certainly come under pressure from the PRG in its attempt to broaden the role of the state and cooperative sectors in the national economy. But few expropriations or nationalisations had actually taken place, and instead the PRG had sought to form a pragmatic working relationship with the private sector in what the NJM strategists saw as an early phase in the process of 'socialist orientation'. They wanted first to eradicate the mismanagement of Gairyism and modernise the economy through an alliance with the business sector rather than pressing ahead with a full-scale socialist transformation. The PRG's pragmatism won approval from the World Bank and the International Monetary Fund, even though most large landowners and merchants limited themselves to the minimum of cooperation with the government. Consequently, the economic elite survived the PRG years and saw the US invasion as a chance to restore its political fortunes.

A significant degree of support for Gairy had also survived the revolution. This was perhaps more surprising, given his controversial human rights record during the 1960s and 1970s and given that his natural supporters — the poorest sections of the rural population — had benefited most from the PRG's programme of social reforms. Nevertheless, loyalty to Gairy apparently remained firm, particularly among older people in rural areas and those who owed their smallholdings to his highly partisan 'agrarian reform'.

Despite the radical project and the impressive achievements of the PRG, the old political forces therefore reemerged more or less intact. This phenomenon, together with the popularity of the PRG's reforms, was to create a serious constraint on US ambitions for Grenada. Neither Blaize's parochial conservatism nor Gairy's reactionary personality cult was the appropriate vehicle for US plans, while the majority of Grenadians were still attracted to the social programme of the PRG. What was clearly needed was a political force in Grenada that could bring in the modernisation and restructuring that the US planned for the island. For the US, that force was to prove elusive.

The last chapter of *Grenada: Whose Freedom?*, published by the Latin America Bureau early in 1984, concluded by predicting that the victors of October 1983 would face serious problems:

> Although the crises of October 1983 were without parallel in the modern history of Grenada and had a considerable impact on Caribbean politics, those who have emerged victorious are left with a major challenge. If they are to provide for the genuine welfare of this little island they will have to do much more than simply act according to a constitution, which itself has already proved to be very difficult for them. As time passes the promises and achievements of those who invaded and those who benefited from the invasion will be judged against the limited but real

advances made between March 1979 and October 1983. This is especially the case for the younger generation, whose expectations were awakened in a manner that a determinedly pro-US system is not even concerned to match. Although it appears extremely unlikely, it is conceivable that the US will make Grenada a 'showcase' by ploughing in vast quantities of aid, but even if this were done it would not break the legacy of centuries of economic backwardness and would be likely only to reinforce external ties of dependence and an internal imbalance of wealth and power.

These predictions have been proven to be well founded. The social, economic and political challenges that have confronted the US and its local allies have been at least as acute as anticipated by critics of the invasion. Far from becoming a showcase of free enterprise virtues in the Caribbean, Grenada now stands more as an example of the limitations and weaknesses of such an approach to development.

* Almost every published analysis of the Grenadian revolution's demise places ultimate responsibility with the NJM faction associated with Bernard Coard. Variously interpreted as an act of personal ambition on the part of Coard himself, an 'ultraleft' putsch, or a combination of both, the move by the pro-Coard majority faction of the NJM Central Committee to reduce the extent of Maurice Bishop's executive power and to introduce so-called 'collective leadership' is usually seen as leading to the final internal crisis of the party, if not to the murders of 19 October 1983. Books and articles by Carew, Lewis, Marable, O'Shaughnessy, Thorndike and others all subscribe to the view that Coard's bid to win greater political control of the revolution resulted in the end of that very process (see *Further Reading*).

As yet, no coherent apologia for the 'Coardite' interpretation of events has appeared, although individuals and groups, in Britain, the US and the Caribbean, have been active in defence of Bernard and Phyllis Coard and the other defendants in the Maurice Bishop murder trial and the subsequent appeal (see p.102). Official statements from the NJM (UK) have lamented the 'tragic events of October 1983' and refer to Maurice Bishop as a 'hero', while Leon Cornwall — a member of the Revolutionary Military Council that took power after the massacre and subsequently condemned to death for his alleged part in those events — has described Bishop as 'a genuine revolutionary democrat and anti-imperialist fighter'.

On the exact circumstances surrounding Bishop's death, however, the existing NJM and its supporters have remained silent, condemning the trial of Coard *et al* as a US-sponsored 'kangaroo court'. Statements ascribed to the NJM in Grenada in the first half of 1989 alluded to 'mistakes' made in the handling of the internal party crisis of October 1983, while a pamphlet written in captivity by Bernard Coard and published in Britain in late 1989 implicitly defends the NJM Central Committee proposal for 'joint leadership' against what is described as the 'massive cultism' surrounding Bishop's leadership. As yet, however, no overall account of the political argument and its violent denouement has yet emerged from this quarter.

Chapter 1
Made in the USA

'These places can't get along without outside investment, outside technology.
Alone, they are not viable; they will in the end have to become something like
offshore states of the United States.'
Peter Johnson, director of Caribbean/Central American Action, 1984.

'It's a lovely piece of real estate.'
George Shultz, on arriving in Grenada, February 1984.

Personnel from the United States Agency for International
Development (USAID) arrived in Grenada 'almost in conjunction with
the troops', stated Peter McPherson, the USAID administrator at a
press conference on 8 November 1983. When asked about the
relationship between the military action and USAID's role in the
island, McPherson replied that 'the Department of Defense people and
the AID people have been working closely, really together, as a team'.
The initial 'disaster-assistance survey team' was soon joined by a larger
mission, made up of representatives from the State Department, the
Department of Commerce and the Overseas Private Investment
Corporation (OPIC). Its brief was to examine how US assistance could
best be directed towards the Grenadian private sector and how US
private investment could be attracted to the island. The appearance
of USAID thus marked the beginning of Grenada's return to a
free-market economy and a political doctrine of private enterprise.

USAID: assistance and profitability

The political aims of USAID are succinctly expressed by former deputy
administrator, Frank M. Coffin in an interview from the late 1970s:

'Our basic, broadest goal is a long-range political one. It is not development for the sake of sheer development . . . An important objective is to open up the maximum opportunity for domestic private initiative and enterprise and to insure that foreign private investment, particularly from the United States, is welcomed and well treated . . . The fostering of a vigorous and expanding private sector in the less developed countries is one of our most important responsibilities . . . Politically, a strong and progressive private business community provides a powerful force for stable responsible Government and a built-in check against Communist dogma.'

Source: Noam Chomsky, *Human Rights and American Foreign Policy*, 1978.

The arrival of USAID staff also signalled the end of a four-year economic boycott by Washington against Grenada. During that time USAID had been active elsewhere in the Caribbean, playing a major role in the economies of Haiti and Jamaica. In nearby Dominica it had tried to privatise the banana industry, while there and in St Lucia it had encouraged US investment in agro-industries and electronics assembly plants. Grenada, however, had been excluded from such assistance. In 1980, in the aftermath of Hurricane Allen, Grenada was refused aid to reconstruct its banana industry. USAID meanwhile allotted grants to Dominica, St Lucia and St Vincent, the other three Windward Island banana producers, for exactly the same purpose. The aid boycott formed part of a wider economic attack; on the day of McPherson's press conference, it was revealed that the US had unsuccessfully opposed Grenada's application for a US$14.1 million loan from the IMF three months earlier.

In the wake of the invasion, however, USAID was anxious to demonstrate the Reagan administration's financial largesse. Such was the flow of funds that by the end of 1983 Grenada briefly became the highest per capita recipient of US economic aid in the world, having been authorised initial grants of US$18.5 million (or nearly 20 per cent of the island's 1982 Gross Domestic Product). Ironically, much of this money was allocated towards repairing damage incurred during the invasion or replacing aid from other sources. A US$3.4 million emergency grant went to repair damage to the water system, roads and other public facilities that had suffered from the US bombardment or heavy military transport equipment.

Other resources were directed towards filling the gaps left by the disruption of the PRG's social programme. Food supplies were needed to continue temporarily the free monthly distribution of powdered milk and butter, while personnel and money were urgently required to replace Cuban health and education workers expelled from the island. Some Grenadians were understandably eager to take advantage of USAID's offer to compensate for war damages; after several speculative claims, US officials testily announced that PRA personnel would not be compensated for injuries and damage incurred in fighting the US invasion force.

From the outset, much money was therefore devoted to continuing existing programmes undertaken by the PRG or simply returning the island to some sort of normality. The irony was not lost on USAID staff who were naturally hostile to the policies of the PRG but were now seemingly financing and administering its commitments. Perhaps the greatest irony, however, was USAID's posture on the construction of Grenada's international airport. At the November press conference, Peter McPherson had insisted that the US government had 'no plans' to complete the airport's construction. The airport, he argued, was never intended for developing the island's tourist industry and would be prohibitively expensive to run.

Within a month the position had changed, largely due to vigorous lobbying by the Grenada Chamber of Commerce. The White House approved a recommendation that the airport's completion be studied as a possible boost to the Grenadian economy. The recommendation stipulated that the US alone could not fund the project and that other foreign donors were required. By March 1984 these donors had been found, and the White House announced that Britain and Canada would contribute to the costs of the remaining construction. The US share of the bill (approximately US$19 million) would form part of the fiscal year 1984's aid package of US$57 million — a sum equivalent to US$570 for each inhabitant of an island where 1983 per capita income was estimated at US$870.

The fact that the Reagan administration was underwriting the cost of the airport that it had previously condemned as a military threat was a remarkable about face. Having hitherto described the airport as irrelevant to Grenada's economic development, the US was now taking over from where Cuba and other donors had left off. To some degree, this paradox was typical of the confusion and inconsistency that surrounded US aid policy in the island. The real extent of financial assistance, for example, was unclear. While speculation flourished among an expectant Grenadian private sector and media, USAID deputy director Jay Morris insisted that the US$57 million pay-out was only 'a one year bulge'. At the same time, it was clear that USAID envisaged at least medium-term support for infrastructural and other programmes as a means of winning Grenadian 'hearts and minds'.

Jim Rudin

Cuban construction team at work on runway of new international airport

Jim Rudin

Sir Paul Scoon officially opens airport, 1984

Was not USAID, according to Peter McPherson, 'firmly committed to the economic recovery and long-term development of Grenada'? But an extended programme of economic aid, in turn, was hardly compatible with the Reagan administration's much-publicised faith in the free market, for, as Fred Halliday put it, 'direct aid was not part of the true gospel of privatization'.

Grenada's Airport: A Change of Heart

'Grenada is building a new naval base, a new air base, storage bases and barracks for troops, and training grounds. And, of course, one can believe that they are all there to export nutmeg . . . It is not nutmeg that is at stake in Central America and the Caribbean, it is the United States' national security.' President Reagan, March 1983.

'The question of completing the airport is very much on everybody's mind and it was discussed everywhere I went . . . We expect to come to a conclusion about it soon. I must say, having landed here and looked around a little, it certainly is needed here and in one way or another, it will be completed.' George Shultz, February 1984.

More ominous for the eager Grenadian business community was US chargé d'affaires Charles Gillespie's hope that 'in a couple of years we'll be able to treat Grenada in the same way as the others in the Eastern Caribbean.' From these others, meanwhile, were coming the first signs of jealousy over Grenada's anticipated windfall. Dominica's Eugenia Charles, for example, complained that an island had to be invaded before it could expect US aid. The dilemma was therefore this: to show that the US could match or even better the aid provided to the PRG from socialist and other sources, while at the same time reducing any future Grenadian government's commitment to state-led development and discouraging dependency on US aid. USAID's 1984 'Country Development Strategy Statement' voiced fears of such dependency and of wider regional resentment:

Decisions made by the USG [US Government] in the near future in determining both the amount of and approach to development assistance will play a major role in the future economic development of Grenada. For example, continued bilateral assistance to Grenada of anything approaching current levels, would most likely result in a 'client state' relationship with the United States — which is neither in the best interests of Grenada nor the USG . . . What is required in Grenada is development of a model of progress which successfully consolidates the return of Grenada to a democratically-based free enterprise-orientated nation, and does so without Grenada becoming so disproportionately economically favoured *vis-a-vis* the rest of the Eastern Caribbean as to generate unmeetable demands and expectations on US resources on the part of other OECS states, which, if unmet, could give rise there to the very sort of problems which we seek to avoid in general.

Private Sector Salvation

For all its apparent inconsistencies, USAID's policy in Grenada was based on two central ideological beliefs. The first was that the PRG had led the island towards economic ruin by an inefficient and repressive emphasis on state intervention. According to a USAID briefing document of January 1986, 'doctrinaire "Marxist" economic policies had discouraged domestic and foreign private investment, infrastructure had been sadly neglected, human rights ignored, and many Grenadians possessing critical skills had emigrated.' The recommended antidote was a substantial injection of private investment and a radical reduction in the state's economic role.

A USAID-led Government Inter-Agency report of December 1983, entitled 'Prospects for Growth in Grenada: the Role of the Private Sector' outlined the basis of this policy. Historically, it noted, the private sector had always played the major role in Grenada, starting during the early colonial period: 'The private sector emerged early in Grenada's history when trading ships from Europe brought articles for sale or barter with the islanders in return for products to be taken back to Europe.' Sensibly omitting the slave trade from this line of analysis, the report went on to identify certain key areas in the post-PRG Grenadian economy which required urgent restructuring. These included the proliferation of state-owned and state-managed enterprises, price controls and state-run marketing of imports, unfavourable investment and tax codes and prohibitive labour legislation. The solution, the report claimed, lay in widespread deregulation, the privatisation of many state-owned businesses, new tax and industrial relations provisions and the replacement of centralised price and import controls by private competition. In short, what was recommended was a dose of what was then known as 'Reaganomics'.

There was little time to be lost. With the formation of the Interim Advisory Council on 15 November 1983, the machinery was in place for the enactment of USAID policies. US advisors and consultants were attached to ministries with the task of overseeing the dismantling of the state sector, while a committee was established to consider the viability of all publicly owned corporations. The first casualties included the Spice Isle Agro-Industry Plant, already damaged by bombing (or, some claimed, deliberate vandalism during the invasion) which the PRG had set up to process agricultural surpluses into a range of food products. With its closure went 70 full-time jobs and work for many more casual labourers. The coffee-processing plant was also closed, as was the Sandino prefabricated housing factory which had commenced operations in March 1983 with an anticipated annual output of 400 housing units. USAID drew up a further list of state-owned enterprises to be closed and perhaps sold: the printing works, the central garage, a carpentry department, and the national telephone and electricity companies.

USAID and the Advisory Council also targeted the cooperative sector which had received special support from the PRG. Under the umbrella of the National Cooperative Development Agency (NACDA), the PRG had encouraged the formation of cooperatives in agriculture, crafts and retailing. This sector, while never matching government expectations, was nevertheless important in generating employment, particularly among young people in rural areas. Largely funded by foreign agencies, the para-statal cooperative movement was an ideologically important, if economically chequered, feature of the PRG's development strategy. Under USAID pressure, however, the Advisory Council closed down NACDA, sacking some staff and transferring others to a minor division of the Ministry of Agriculture. Funds for new cooperative ventures were frozen, while existing projects were gradually allowed to fall into disrepair.

In a parallel policy shift, the state-owned Grenada Farms Corporation (GFC) was singled out for immediate privatisation. In the first part of 1984, eight of the existing 38 state farms (totalling 2,887 acres out of 8,815 acres) were returned to private ownership. This move was much more ideological than practical, since several of the farms in question had been taken into state control precisely because their owners had neglected them. USAID was also labouring under the misapprehension that the GFC managed land primarily expropriated and nationalised by the PRG on political grounds. Not surprisingly, there were few takers for the farms, and those larger owners who claimed their land hoped to resell it to the government at a future date. Similar developments occurred in the tourism sector, where the PRG had taken control of several hotels and other facilities that had become economically unviable or had already been run by the Gairy regime. Private purchasers were immediately invited to take over.

Jobs in the public sector were quickly destroyed by this approach. The PRA, of course, had been disbanded at once, putting perhaps 600, mainly young, Grenadians out of full-time work. They were joined by hundreds of government employees as the US authorities and then the Advisory Council sought to cut the public-sector wage bill. Ministries particularly associated with the PRG's social programme were special targets; these included Mobilisation, Culture, Women's Affairs and Education. As PRG programmes were abruptly cut, so unemployment soared. Purges of PRG supporters in the civil service and wholesale redundancies cost an estimated 3,000 jobs within the first year of US control (see p.77).

The crusade against the state sector thus included closures, sackings and piecemeal privatisation. It also meant using political pressure to starve existing publicly owned enterprises of funds from other sources. Washington persuaded multilateral lending agencies such as the Inter-American Development Bank and the Caribbean Development Bank to block loans aimed at financing or improving the public sector. 'There is a lot of pressure, from the highest level, not to lend to the Grenadian government for the rehabilitation of these state-owned enterprises', said Marius St Rose, chief economist at the Caribbean Development Bank, in an interview in early 1984. 'There is a lot of pressure to make Grenada a totally unregulated economy', he added.

AIFLD: Labour Pains

One of the principal elements of USAID policy in the Caribbean region has always been the encouragement of trade unions which are receptive to the idea of private sector-led development. The American Institute for Free Labor Development (AIFLD) exists precisely to form and support such trade unions and is widely seen as one of the more politically active agents of US regional policy. During the PRG regime, accusations of destabilisation and subversion were often made against AIFLD in Grenada. At the same time, the PRG period saw a huge increase in trade union membership, activity and influence in the island. The percentage of the agricultural, industrial and commercial workforce belonging to unions rose from 40 to 80 (although many members did not pay regular dues), while new unions emerged to replace the corrupt and conservative organisations that had been controlled by Eric Gairy and his supporters. The collapse of the revolution, however, triggered a crisis in Grenadian trade unionism. Not only were two prominent union leaders — Vincent Noel and Fitzroy Bain — murdered in the massacre of 19 October 1983, but the ensuing invasion opened the way for an attempted onslaught by AIFLD and its Grenadian allies.

AIFLD

AID has also played an important role in subverting popular organizations in order to moderate their demands and effectiveness. This has mostly been carried out in close collaboration with AIFLD, another institution set up in 1961 by the American trade union confederation, the AFL-CIO, made up of business, labour and government representatives and chaired by that ubiquitous committee figure, J. Peter Grace [president of the giant multinational W.R. Grace and Co.] AID and AIFLD, both closely linked to the CIA and often used as vehicles for its clandestine operations, are two more instruments of US foreign policy. AIFLD has been very active in Central America and the Caribbean, attempting to subvert and coopt the labour movement in the region . . . In Guyana in the early 1960s, while it was still a British colony, AIFLD participated in a CIA campaign to overthrow the government of Cheddi Jagan.

Source: Jenny Pearce, *Under the Eagle,* p.45

The USAID report of December 1983 merely confirmed what Maurice Bishop had claimed and the US had denied for the past four years: that AIFLD, although not openly operating in the island, had been collaborating with right-wing union leaders in revolutionary Grenada. The report observed that 'AIFLD maintained close contacts with these groups during the Bishop years and is on the scene now.' Conservative union bosses such as Eric Pierre of the Seamen's and Waterfront Workers Union (SWWU) who had opposed every aspect of the PRG's labour policies were now instrumental in AIFLD's post-invasion campaign. This involved discrediting the PRG and its achievements, leading an anti-communist attack within the labour movement and attempting to weaken militant trade unions by poaching members.

The overall aim was the restructuring of Grenadian trade unionism and the replacement of progressive leaders with pro-US, pro-private sector activists. To this end, AIFLD and the SWWU organised seminars on 'Political Theories and Systems' (a crash course in anti-communism) for potential right-wing unionists. Disinformation was used to spread the impression that various unions had collapsed completely, thereby allowing small groups to take control at small, unpublicised meetings. Intimidation and propaganda were directed against trade unionists identified with the PRG. Conservatives, on the other hand, enjoyed considerable support from AIFLD and USAID, which, according to reports, had allocated a budget of US$1.4 million for this work. A British labour movement delegation which visited the island in December 1983 recorded '[attempts] by American-trained and backed Grenadians to remove elected Union officers and take over some unions.' One group of AIFLD-supported trade unionists tried to take over the leadership of the Technical and Allied Workers Union (TAWU). According to the British report: 'rank-and-file members of the union to whom we spoke claimed that this group was being organised by the AIFLD-trained Grenadian who had just returned to Grenada from the United States.'

The arrival in Grenada of Charlie Wood in early 1984 marked the beginning of AIFLD infiltration of the agricultural sector. Wood, an AIFLD official, at once tried to take advantage of the crisis within the Agricultural and General Workers Union (AGWU). AGWU had been led by Fitzroy Bain, a leading supporter of Maurice Bishop, and had become one of Grenada's most influential and dynamic unions, largely superseding Gairy's conservative GMMIWU (changed from GMMWU in 1975) as the representative of rural labour. With Bain's death, the RMC coup and the invasion, the AGWU disintegrated. For USAID and the Advisory Council, the union nevertheless represented a radical and hence undesirable rallying point for agricultural workers, and Wood was given the task of founding an alternative union that would further weaken AGWU. In March 1984, he established the Agricultural and Allied Workers Union (AAWU), lavishly funded by US agencies.

Wood's campaign was short-lived, however. By September 1985, most of AAWU's officers and members had resigned, complaining that Wood had simply set up a thinly disguised employers' union made up of small farmers with little real inclination towards trade unionism. When the AIFLD official tried to persuade his membership to accept wage decreases, the US-sponsored union finally collapsed, many of the rank-and-file membership opting for Gairy's rival union. As a result, GMMIWU regained some of the ground it had lost since 1979 and was able to organise effective strikes in 1986. Subsequent unions singled out for AIFLD-inspired takeovers include TAWU and the Grenada Union of Teachers (GUT) in an attempt to gain influence in the Trade Union Council (TUC).

The destabilisation of Grenada's trade union movement and the attempted hijacking of the TUC coincided logically with the hoped-for influx of private US investment. The December 1983 USAID report had recommended that a US Department of Labor expert on the Caribbean Basin Initiative commence discussions with the Grenadian authorities on new labour legislation attuned to US specifications. In other words, the Interim Council was advised to make it clear to potential US investors that trade unions would not affect their profits. The Advisory Council's investment code, published in February 1984, pledged to give the leading role in economic development to the private sector, domestic and foreign. Offering ten-year tax concessions, duty-free benefits and other incentives, the code complemented the unofficial promise to would-be investors that trade unions would not be a problem.

Creating a Climate

In February 1986, the date of Ronald Reagan's triumphal four-hour visit to Grenada, USAID could look back on 26 months of considerable investment and influence in Grenada. In a press release, the organisation claimed to have joined with the Advisory Council and subsequently the elected New National Party (NNP) government (see p.46) 'in an extraordinarily intense and wide-ranging program designed to develop the economic foundation necessary for stable growth to occur'. Noting that financial assistance to Grenada up to January 1986 totalled some US$72.6 million, the statement detailed eight principal areas in which USAID had been active.

Of these areas some were relatively minor in terms of expenditure. The 'Special Development Activities' programme, for instance, had been allocated US$100,000 per year to fund 'community self-help projects', such as small-scale building and repairs. Education assistance, comprising repairs to schools and short- and long-term scholarships for Grenadians to study in the US had cost some US$2 million. 'Project Hope', a USAID-administered health programme designed to replace the Cuban-supported primary health care of the PRG, had received a budget of US$2.1 million, supported by private contributions of US$1.3 million in medical equipment and supplies.

Others were more capital-intensive. The new international airport had cost US$19 million to complete, while an additional US$6 million

Philip Wolmuth

Roadside notice, St George's, 1984

had been directed towards other infrastructural development, including road repairs, water and electricity supply and the construction of factory shells. USAID's bid to privatise the agricultural sector had cost approximately US$2.8 million, while a further US$17 million had been spent on what the press release described as 'fiscal and other policy reforms'. These included restoring liquidity to commercial banks to enable private-sector borrowing, filling budget shortfalls and restructuring the relationship between the state and private business. This last category of reform was perhaps the most drastic alteration to the Grenadian economy undertaken by USAID. The famous euphemism of 'policy dialogue' (meaning conditionality) suggests that this was the price paid by Grenada's government for USAID's assistance. The release noted:

> Reforms resulting from policy dialogue associated with this assistance have included: (1) liberalization of import licensing requirements; (2) development of a program to privatize major state-owned enterprises, commencement of divestiture of government-owned agricultural lands, and transfer of management of the principal commodity associations to the

private sector; (3) rationalization of the public sector investment program; (4) commencement of a fiscal (budgetary and tax) reform program; (5) revision of the investment code; (6) interest rate ceilings raised; (7) removal of price controls on domestically produced items; (8) elimination of the import monopoly on cement; and (9) relaxation of foreign exchange controls.

The social and economic impact of these measures is discussed in greater detail in Chapter 3. Their political significance lies in the fact that USAID and the US administration were enjoying extraordinary influence in the policies and practice of an ostensibly independent and sovereign government. This influence extended into every major area of economic development. Just as structures and organisations established by the PRG were dismantled, so a new USAID-funded bureaucracy was set up to implement Washington's plans:

* The National Development Foundation (NDF): aimed to assist small individual entrepreneurs with technical assistance and financing in a move diametrically opposed to the PRG's emphasis on cooperative development. The NDF was one of a number of such bodies established by USAID in the Eastern Caribbean and was centrally administered from a regional headquarters in Barbados.
    * The Industrial Development Corporation (IDC): established in January 1985 on the advice of a USAID-financed report from the management consultants Coopers and Lybrand. The IDC was intended to facilitate foreign investment, with a full-time USAID advisor seconded to it. It was also used by USAID to reduce the government's role in such investment, shifting authority from the cabinet to this new body.

Other pro-private sector organisations included the International Executive Service Corps, funded by USAID to provide technical assistance resources (largely in the form of advice from retired US executives) to local businesses, the USAID-assisted Caribbean Financial Services Corporation (a regional investment credit agency), Caribbean/Central American Action (CCAA — a corporate business-funded organisation aiming to assist the regional private sector) and the Caribbean Association of Industry and Commerce (CAIC — a USAID-funded group concerned with training and lobbying in favour of privatisation).

US Agencies in Grenada and the Caribbean

US Government Agencies

USAID: US Agency for International Development. Administers US government foreign assistance programmes, ranging from road-building to cash injections for friendly governments.
AIFLD: American Institute for Free Labor Development. Largely USAID funded body which sets up, trains and funds labour organisations which support private sector-led development.
OPIC: Overseas Private Investment Corporation. Insures US private companies against foreign investment risks in particular countries and otherwise encourages private investment under pro-US governments
CBIC: Caribbean Basin Information Center. Attached to US Department of Commerce. Encourages US businesses to invest and trade with the region, under the terms of the Caribbean Basin Initiative.

US Government-funded Agencies

NED: National Endowment for Democracy. Set up by President Reagan in 1983 with a US$18m grant for its first year. Nominally non-government, but 100 per cent government funded. Funds pro-US trade union organisations, media (eg *La Prensa* in Nicaragua) and research institutes.
IESC: International Executive Service Corps. Set up by USAID to provide technical advice to local businesses in the Caribbean from retired US executives.

US Non Governmental and Private Sector Agencies

Project Hope: Approximately 50% USAID-funded right-wing aid agency specialising in health care. Controversial track record in Vietnam and Central America.
CCAA: Caribbean/Central American Action. Funded by US corporations and individuals. Founded in 1980 to encourage US trade with the region and build links between regional and US private sectors. Works closely with USAID.

USAID-funded Caribbean Agencies

CFEC: Caribbean Financial Services Corporation. Regional investment credit agency.
CAIC: Caribbean Association of Industry and Commerce. Builds up chambers of commerce and manufacturers' associations throughout the region. USAID-funded and CCAA-dominated.

USAID-funded Grenadian Organisations

NDF: National Development Foundation. Assists small entrepreneurs with technical assistance and financing.
IDC: Industrial Development Corporation. Set up in 1985 to encourage foreign investment.

Tax policy was very largely determined by USAID specialists. The controversial abolition of income tax in the budget of February 1986 and the shift to Value Added Tax (VAT) were carried out on their advice. USAID staff had seen the existing tax system as inefficient, open to abuse and a disincentive to private enterprise. The resulting introduction of indirect tax was intended to boost revenue and encourage growth. However, it also shifted the burden of taxation from the incomes of the rich onto the basic goods consumed by rich and poor alike, with catastrophic effects on the most deprived sectors of Grenadian society.

Yet relations between USAID and the Grenadian government were soon to sour, especially over the government's reluctance to implement fully the USAID-approved tax reform. A USAID spokesperson maintained in June 1988 that its goals would have been achieved had it not been for the tinkering of the Grenadian government which insisted on a string of exemptions and 'special cases' within the new tax system. As it was, its failure to generate expected tax revenue forced USAID to make up the government's revenue shortfalls from its 'Economic Support Fund' (US$12 million 1984-5) and 'Structural Adjustment Program' (US$11 million 1986-7) grants. In a 1990 'Regional Development Strategy' paper USAID lamented that 'Grenada . . . has carried out extensive fiscal reforms, but uneven (and to some extent imprudent) implementation has resulted in financing gaps, supported in part by AID.'

'Retrenchment' or the large-scale sackings of public sector workers was also intended as an intrinsic part of the USAID project. The initial study of the civil service by the UK management consultancy firm, Peat, Marwick and Mitchell, was financed by the British government, but USAID advisors oversaw the programme of redundancies. Here, too, the government's achievements fell short of US expectations; despite an initial onslaught on PRG supporters, the public sector failed to shrink sufficiently, since government loyalists were hired to replace sacked workers. Three years after the retrenchment programme began,

USAID officials admitted that it had solved little and recognised the political dangers of increasing unemployment still further.

The selling-off of state-owned enterprises continued apace. USAID saw the agricultural and tourism sectors as the most promising targets for privatisation. The GFC which the Advisory Council had already started to split up was further dismantled. Under USAID pressure, the government cancelled a Caribbean Development Bank loan of US$2.7 million which was intended to modernise the public-sector farms. In place of state-owned estates USAID first proposed returning the land to large-scale private agri-businesses. When this policy failed, it advocated a system of 'model farms', to be rented or owned by small private farmers. With the help of a US$400,000 USAID grant, properties of varying sizes were earmarked for lease or sale, while subsidised fertiliser was distributed to farmers engaged in private banana and cocoa production. Grenada Dairies was also privatised, sold to a Jamaican businessman for the low price of US$20,000, while control of the state-run Telescope Quarry was snapped up by a private US concern.

In tourism, two of the hotels managed by the state-run Grenada Resorts Corporation were privatised, despite government attempts to sell off more. Most controversial was the decision to lease the 183-room Grenada Beach Hotel to a Canadian-based company. Owned by a Trinidadian millionaire, Issa Nicholas, Isgrad International arranged for the US company Ramada Inns to manage the hotel, while paying the Grenadian government one per cent of gross revenue or a minimum of US$50,000 per year. The government further guaranteed a loan of US$7.1 million from the International Finance Corporation to allow Nicholas to refurbish the hotel. Critics pointed out that the government was selling itself very short, since the PRG had already invested at least US$500,000 in the hotel since buying it from Holiday Inn after an accidental fire.

Investors' Paradise?

The attempted remoulding of Grenada's economy was based on one central expectation: that foreign private investment, notably from the US, would be the engine for growth and development. The Reagan administration made every effort to attract this investment, employing several organisations to identify prospective individuals and businesses, as well as encouraging Grenadian entrepreneurs. Weeks after the invasion, the White House and CCAA sponsored a visit by a 'private-sector survey team', during which Peter Johnson explained the benefits to be gained from the CBI and other US regional programmes. In January 1984, the Office of Private Sector Initiatives of the White House organised a trip to Grenada for fifteen US executives, interested in investment opportunity. The Grenada Chamber of Commerce had already been sent by USAID to the November 1983 Miami Conference on the Caribbean, organised by CCAA as a trade fair for the region. Other para-governmental and related agencies such as the Caribbean Basin Information Center (attached to the US Department of Commerce), the Export-Import Bank and OPIC were also involved in promoting the island. These efforts continued through 1985 and 1986, and more sporadically afterwards.

At first, rumours of massive US investment circulated in Grenada. The local press reported enthusiastically each visit by USAID-sponsored business organisations and would-be entrepreneurs, and public pronouncements by George Shultz and Vice-President Bush were calculated to keep levels of optimism high. The hotel sector was especially expected to benefit from an influx of foreign capital, and press reports and government statements linked companies such as Hyatt and Sheraton with the island. Other reports spoke of Hong Kong investors and the so-called Caribbean Consortium that was preparing to build a 250-room hotel and further facilities. Little or nothing of this ever materialised, however. Some local and regional investment did take place, particularly in small-scale tourist development, and several small factories opened, financed by Trinidadian or Grenadian business concerns. Neal and Massy, Trinidad's largest conglomerate, opened a soft drink factory in April 1984, creating 30 jobs, while other factories were established in garment production and light engineering. What employment was created was tiny in comparison to the jobs lost in the dismantling of the state sector.

Such US investors as were attracted by the generous investment incentives and get-rich-quick atmosphere were often incompetent or, in several cases, crooked. A company established to market one-fifth of Grenada's 1984 nutmeg crop to the US market collapsed within months, despite having been strongly supported by the US authorities. It left debts to the Grenada Nutmeg Cooperative Association of over US$20,000. Equally short-lived was a toy factory, set up by one William H Ingle in 1984. Ingle claimed he had US$4 million worth of orders for his wooden toys, and that his 85 Grenadian employees were content with their weekly wage of US$40. By early 1985, however, Ingle-Grenada Ltd went bankrupt, owing more than US$200,000 to local banks. When examined more closely by US officials, it was discovered that Ingle had dishonestly obtained US$350,000 in loans from OPIC by pretending to have a US$200,000 certificate of deposit as collateral. When sentenced by a US federal court for fraud, Ingle claimed that the White House and OPIC had overlooked irregularities in their eagerness to see the scheme started. 'Reagan phoned me', stated Ingle, 'and said we could come here to Grenada and show how free enterprise works.'

The chapter of fiascos has continued to the present day. After months of anticipation and government propaganda it was announced in January 1988 that the so-called Grenada International Service Corporation (GISCO) had failed to meet a deadline for concrete proposals on its investment. Plans for US$70 million of investment in an executive jet service and hotel construction had raised government hopes of significant employment in construction; after the event, USAID claimed to have warned the Grenadian government that the company was economically unviable. The government had meanwhile unquestioningly leased state-owned Crown Lands to GISCO, declining to debate the issue in parliament. Other debacles have included the collapse of Rigid Panel (the private successor to the Sandino prefabricated housing plant) and the disastrous record of Discovery TV, a private channel run by a prominent US supporter of the NNP government.

Excuses for the lamentable level of US investment had to be found. The first was that it would not arrive until the Interim Advisory Council had been replaced by a more permanent political structure. In July 1984, US chargé d'affaires Loren Lawrence told the *New York Times* that 'very little of the American investment money that we hope to see come here will actually come here until there's an elected government.' The election, however, changed little. Blame was then laid with the PRG, when in 1986, USAID was forced to report:

> Foreign and private investment for the first two years following the rescue mission has lagged behind optimistic expectations due to the legacy of economic, political, and institutional constraints inherited from the previous regime. Nevertheless, substantial progress has been made in terms of systems and infrastructure in place and policy initiatives launched. This has set the stage for dramatic improvements in development activity and growth over the next few years.

Finally, the problem was seen as one of bureaucratic obstruction on the part of the Grenadian authorities. A December 1987 report by the IDC complained that potential investors were 'left alone to walk the bureaucratic maze unguided and unattended', pointing out that businesses wishing to lease government land or factory space had to

Jim Rudin

Signs appealing for US investment await George Bush, March 1985

deal with at least four separate ministries. By now, tension between the USAID-run IDC and the government had grown, to the point that USAID was blaming the Grenadian administration for lack of foreign investment as well as chronic budgetary shortfalls (see p.52).

The IDC nevertheless issued positive statements for three consecutive years, claiming that hundreds of enquiries had been received from would-be US investors. Yet few ever took shape. Investment missions became increasingly desperate and were occasionally embarrassingly unsuccessful. By 1990, only four significant US investors had arrived in Grenada. Subsidiaries of SmithKline Beckman, Abbott Laboratories, Shering/Plough and Johnson and Johnson were operating in the purpose-built US$1.8 million factory area at Frequente, producing pharmaceutical items (surgical gloves and contact lens cases) and employing just 200 local workers.

The Investment Mission

The Reagan administration's attempts to woo US investors to Grenada were dogged by incompetence and indifference. Steve Fassihi, a US businessman who has since started a small company in the island, describes his experience:

'The investment mission was put together by the Private Initiative Office at the White House and was handled by a public relations firm. The trip was postponed so many times that a few of my business friends who were very much interested in being part of the White House mission gave up on it, as it was logistically so disastrous. It was supposed to happen in June 1986, but didn't actually take place until September, and only three people, including me, came down to Grenada. None of these people were decision makers; one was a junior vice-president who wanted to come and grow some herbs to sell in New York City, one was from the South, whose aim was to set up a sweatshop in the garment business, and the third was a gentleman in transportation or something similar. But the sad part is — and I have my notes from the meeting — that there were twenty-nine people, including virtually the whole Grenadian cabinet, sitting in the conference room at the Ramada Renaissance hotel. It was embarrassing. The entire American mission in Grenada, from Barbados, people like the vice-chairman of the Republican Party, people from the White House were all there. The mission was disastrous. There was a party given by Mr Jack Leary, the chargé d'affaires, paid for, of course, by the American taxpayer, and I have a list of the guests. About 125 people, everybody in the Grenadian government, all the business leaders, and only two people went as the so-called White House investment mission. I didn't go because I was too embarrassed. On the following night, we were supposed to have a dinner in honour of the investors who came to Grenada at the Prime Minister's house. The situation was so bad that it was cancelled, and the excuse was that it was rainy weather.'

Source: Interview, July 1988

More than six years after the invasion, it had become amply apparent that Grenada was not to become the investors' paradise that some had hoped. In late 1983, Ted Morse, USAID's director on the island had boasted: 'investors want elections, security and infrastructure: we will give all three'. Elections and improved infrastructure had been delivered, but security — or at least a confidence-inspiring image of it — had not. USAID officials privately admitted that US investors still saw Grenada as a 'hot spot', where Cuban guerrillas still roamed the hills. Negative press reports about the NNP government's political collapse after 1988 hardly improved Grenada's troubled image.

Furthermore, the island offered nothing particularly enticing to investors, once the political hyperbole of the Reagan administration had faded. Not only was its location at the bottom of the Antillean chain inconvenient for US markets, but its labour force was seen as less industrious than those of Singapore or Hong Kong and more expensive and potentially militant than those of Haiti or the Dominican Republic. 'Grenada is not a goldmine for anyone', admitted a USAID representative in June 1988.

Return to Obscurity

As Grenada's political symbolism has gradually faded in the eyes of the US public, so too has its claim to special treatment from Washington, increasingly concerned by its own vast budget deficit and the threat of the Gramm-Rudman congressional legislation that proposes compulsory departmental cuts if voluntary savings are not made. After the high point of 1984, US financial assistance dwindled to approximately US$15 million per year for the period 1986-7. This meant that Grenada was no longer receiving significantly higher levels of bilateral aid than other Eastern Caribbean territories. In the fiscal year 1988, USAID provided no more than US$7 million to Grenada, of which US$3.8 million went directly to help the deficit-plagued budget.

US policy has been to withdraw gradually and, in the words of USAID officials, to 'wean the Grenadian government off American aid'. This involves pushing Grenada away from a bilateral 'special relationship' and towards such multilateral agencies as the IMF and the World Bank which can impose their own conditions on loans to Grenada. In particular, USAID has been anxious to steer Grenada towards the so-called Tighter Consultative Group, a subcommittee of the Caribbean Group for Cooperation in Economic Development — itself a creation of the World Bank. The unwillingness of the Grenadian government to submit to the Tighter Consultative Group's conditions has been a source of conflict with USAID. Meanwhile, the first negotiations with the IMF took place in late 1987, but ended inconclusively.

Economic aid from the US increasingly takes the form of regional programmes, directed primarily at private-sector initiatives throughout the Eastern Caribbean which, in US eyes, are more cost-effective than bilateral support. Typical is the Eastern Caribbean Investment Promotion Service (ECIPS), funded by USAID to encourage offshore investment in electronics, clothing manufacturing and data processing.

Aid from other sources, meanwhile, continues to subsidise the Grenadian economy. Canada, for instance, provided funding of C$7 million (US$6 million) to help rehabilitate the ailing cocoa industry (assistance negotiated by the PRG), while a grant of C$7.5 million (US$6.5 million) towards the modernisation of the telephone system was only jeopardised by the government's decision to set up a joint company with the British Cable & Wireless company. Britain has also stepped up its bilateral aid to Grenada, following a virtual embargo during the years of the PRG. In early 1985 the Barbados-based British Development Division announced an aid package of £5 million in grants and loans to be spread over five years. In 1989, the annual British aid package was estimated at approximately £1 million and a slight increase was promised. Other recent donor countries have included Venezuela, South Korea and Taiwan who have provided credit lines and grants, and France which donated FF4 million (US$700,000) in 1988. Japan is also seen as a major potential donor. At the same time, regional and multilateral aid and loans continue to reach the Grenadian government through such agencies as the European Development Fund (EDF), the United Nations Food and Agriculture Organisation (FAO), the Organisation of American States (OAS) and the Caribbean Development Bank (CDB).

Despite such multilateral outside support, the Grenadian government seemed alarmed by the withdrawal of US bilateral aid. In 1985, when it became apparent that USAID's Grenada budget for the following year would be substantially lower than the preceding year's US$57 million, Foreign Minister Ben Jones told a news conference that a sum of US$500 million over the next five years 'might just set us right'. A note of panic was discernible in Prime Minister Herbert Blaize's appeal for further US funding that same January: 'I think we can compare this Grenada situation with the kind of situation that faced Europe after the Second World War . . . We call for a kind of Marshall Plan for Grenada.'

Such appeals largely fell on deaf ears. Although chargé d'affaires Jack Leary soothingly claimed in January 1988 that USAID's programme in Grenada remains 'substantial', it was no secret that by then only one of the five full-time project officers present in 1984 remained. In line with plans, this last USAID project officer left the island in 1989, transferring Grenada-related work to the regional office in Barbados. This last stage of the phased withdrawal signified the end of USAID's direct input into the Grenadian government's economic policies, although it will retain some leverage through intermediary agencies and the allocation of grants.

As USAID closed up shop in Grenada, its staff may well have reflected on the process that has turned the island from a proposed showcase of free market prosperity to an unwelcome burden on the US taxpayer. Had substantial US private investment arrived, the theory of private sector-led development might have been vindicated. As it is, the US has spent approximately US$120 million on preparing the way for a goldrush that never occurred.

For that at least some of the blame lies with USAID and its related US agencies who have sought to impose an inappropriate and expensive blueprint on a vulnerable small island economy. Critics point in particular to the extraordinary priority given to privatisation at any cost, to the extent that a mere seven per cent of USAID expenditure in Grenada has been directed towards education, health, agricultural research and community-based projects. The overwhelming majority of USAID funds have instead gone towards dismantling the state sector, encouraging private enterprise and wooing foreign capital — with negligible success. Another criticism is that USAID's administrative overheads are disproportionately high, with huge costs devoted to consultancies and reports rather than actual projects.

Aiding Consultants

Total AID allocations for social services and basic human needs, including education, health, agricultural research and extension, and community self-help added up to less than 7% of AID spending in Grenada. A rural development worker said, 'We hear over the radio all the time that the United States is giving us so many thousands of dollars for this project or that. But by the time the experts and bureaucrats take their share, we don't see any of it. That's why when people hear these announcements they say "Here comes more of that radio money", because that's all it is —radio money'.

Even in small business promotion, described by AID as a top priority, local enterprise has gotten short shrift. AID allocated $12 million for one project to aid small and medium-sized enterprises in the Eastern Caribbean. Part of the funds was supposed to be channeled to small and 'micro' enterprises through National Development Foundations (NDFs), established under AID guidance. But according to the director of Grenada's NDF, 'AID puts so many conditions on a project that they stifle it. It's as if the people who work for AID don't feel we should get anything, and that their job is to block aid. There is a lot of money paid to Americans for consultant fees, but little for local loans.'

Source: Kathy McAgee, *Hurricane: IMF, World Bank, USAID in the Caribbean*

But responsibility lies to a large extent also with the political rulers of Grenada and their inability to create the climate of stability that acts as a precondition for foreign investment. In particular, factionalism, personal ambition and political intrigue have created an atmosphere of continual crisis, at odds with the aim of improving investors' confidence.

Chapter 2
Party Tricks

'No empire in history conquers a new territory and then evacuates. It sets up a machinery of governance to guarantee its continuing control of the newly conquered province.'
Gordon K. Lewis, *Grenada: The Jewel Despoiled*, 1987

'The military action was the easy part. Now we have the problems.'
Major Douglas Frey, US army spokesman, November 1983

Until 25 October 1983, Sir Paul Scoon, Governor-General of Grenada, was an obscure figure. Appointed by Queen Elizabeth II on the advice of Prime Minister Gairy in 1978, the Governor-General symbolised the island's tenuous links with the former metropole and occupied a largely ceremonial function as representative of the nominal head of state. He outlived the last stage of the Gairy regime, was tolerated by the PRG which saw no advantage in scrapping his post, and survived the brief interregnum of the RMC. His gift for political survival was due to his ability to coexist with whatever regime was in power, irrespective of ideology. To Gordon K. Lewis, he was the 'Uriah Heep of Grenada history', the epitome of the 'obedient and deferential colonial public servant'.

With the US invasion, Scoon was suddenly transformed into an important international figure, even if certain misunderstandings still existed over his identity and role (President Reagan reportedly thought him to be the British Governor of a colonial territory). The reason for this new-found prominence was that the Governor-General had been transformed into *de facto* executive leader of the island. Although the US forces had invaded and occupied Grenada, they could not be openly seen to rule it, and a constitutionally appropriate frontman had to be found. Scoon was the obvious choice, and one of the first tasks of the invasion force was to take him from his residence to the *USS Guam*, where he remained for two days. At the end of that period, on 28 October, a note was produced, ostensibly dated 23 October, requesting outside military assistance via the OECS and thereby retrospectively attempting to legitimise the US action. (Constitutionally, the action was hard to justify, since Scoon had made no appeal for assistance to Britain and had no right to invite an invasion by a foreign power without first consulting the British Queen). Constitutionally dubious and clearly backdated, the note scarcely fitted with Scoon's less rehearsed remark to the *Trinidad Express* that the first he knew of the invasion was when US troops appeared in his garden!

Nevertheless, Scoon was duly installed as nominal ruler of Grenada under the terms of a state of emergency, declared on 31 October, and showed his gratitude by commenting to the press that 'the Americans have done a bloody good job'. Although relishing his position of one-man executive authority, he was soon forced by British and Commonwealth pressure to end the state of emergency on 16 November and to appoint a caretaker administration. This body, known as the Interim Advisory Council, was to run the island until elections could be held. This temporary arrangement marked the first setback for the US political plan for Grenada, which had foreseen the swift installment of a handpicked government, led possibly by Francis Alexis, a favourite of Washington. International opposition, notably from the Commonwealth, blocked this plan and forced the US to settle for a combination of Scoon and the Advisory Council.

The first choice for head of the provisional government was the respected Grenadian economist, Alister McIntyre, but he initially refused the post, partly on grounds of ill health, but also because he did not wish to administer an island under virtual US military control. Scoon then appointed a personal friend, Nicholas Brathwaite, a former head teacher and regional director of the Commonwealth Youth Programme. It was later reported that McIntyre would have accepted the job, under certain conditions, and that one of them being complete executive power, Scoon had moved quickly to block his appointment by selecting Brathwaite.

The Interim Advisory Council was for the most part comprised of Grenadian technocrats and civil servants unconnected to the NJM or PRG, and prepared to work under the dual influence of Scoon and the US authorities. Within a week of its establishment, Anthony Rushford, a British lawyer and author of Grenada's 1974 constitution, resigned from his post of Attorney-General, accusing Scoon of 'total indifference and lack of cooperation' in his unwillingness to disclose the details of his much-publicised request for US assistance. This was hardly surprising, for the real rulers of post-invasion were neither Scoon nor the Interim Advisory Council, but the occupants of the US embassy.

Chief among these initially was Charles 'Tony' Gillespie, the US Deputy Assistant Secretary of State for Caribbean Affairs, a senior State Department official who had played a large part in orchestrating the invasion from the US embassy in Barbados. His task was to oversee the 'normalisation' of Grenada and its transition from military occupation to constitutional government. He and his staff, the Interim Advisory Council and Scoon thus formed a temporary, if unequal, triumvirate. Brathwaite was effectively excluded from the daily meetings between Gillespie (nicknamed locally as 'Sir Paul' Gillespie), Scoon and Major-General Farris, commander of the US forces. Although there were apparently points of conflict between the parties involved, the large amounts of financial aid that the Interim Advisory Council requested and obtained from the US embassy and USAID meant that Scoon generally went along with the US authorities. They, in turn, were also quite happy to bypass Scoon and his appointees altogether on basic matters of policy. When a US Quaker delegation visited Grenada, its members discovered that the Advisory Council had not even been shown the US Inter-Agency report of December 1983 (see p.22) which outlined plans for the island's development.

Such initiatives as the Advisory Council took were certainly approved, if not dictated, by the US officials. They included the dismantling of the state and cooperative sectors in agriculture, the closure of the key state-owned plants and the decision to complete the construction of the international airport. The interim regime also charged the Caribbean Development Bank to explore the feasibility of further, longer-term privatisation programmes. Although criticised as passive and incompetent, the Advisory Council acted as a willing vehicle for US advisors to implement radical changes in the island. The report of the British labour movement delegation in December 1983 remarked that these changes were 'far more all-encompassing and irreversible than most experienced after Western-style elections'. But if many of these were the result of deliberate policy, others, notably the dramatic collapse of the cooperative sector, were also a reflection of the chaos and uncertainty that existed during a military quasi-occupation.

According to Advisory Council member Pat Emmanuel in late November, the interim regime had to 'reject the impression that it is a puppet'. Crucial to this was the rapid removal of US combat troops and their replacement by local and regional security forces. The first objective was quickly realised; on 12 and 13 December, the majority of US troops departed, and the next day most of their equipment left St George's harbour. Left behind were 300 US troops, 200 of whom were deployed as 'military policemen', 100 belonging to the notorious Psychological Operations (PSYOPS) team. They were supported by an enlarged 'Caribbean Peacekeeping Force' (CPF) of some 1000, comprised of 350 Jamaicans and personnel from five other Caribbean territories. With the scaling down of the US military presence, command devolved to a lieutenant-colonel of the Jamaica Defence Force, whose men policed the island with US troops and Grenadian police.

Training commenced immediately with the aim of establishing regular and paramilitary police units on the island. US Green Berets trained members of the paramilitary 80-man Special Service Unit (SSU), while Britain promised £500,000 and staff for the training of regular police officers. An expanded police force of 550 (formerly 200), with membership of the Regional Security System (RSS), was seen as adequate for immediate security purposes. The phased withdrawal took place over the next 18 months. In January 1985, half of the Jamaican contingent left, while the *New York Times* reported that an 80-strong Grenadian SSU unit was ready to be established. In June, all but 30 US 'security specialists' left Grenada.

Marriage of Convenience

Parallel to the gradual removal of foreign troops and their replacement by local security forces was the attempt to reintroduce a constitutional and electoral framework for a return to parliamentary rule. Those who were most enthusiastic about the invasion, notably the business sector, were least eager to see the return of party politics in Grenada. They saw a permanent US military and administrative presence as the best guarantee of Washington's commitment to massive continuing aid. The US attitude was more pragmatic, wishing to reduce responsibilities in Grenada by ensuring that an approved government took office, but realising that certain risks were involved. Chief among these was the possibility that either the remnants of the NJM might gain significant support or, more likely, that Eric Gairy might stage a comeback.

Gairy had returned to Grenada early in 1984. Claiming to be the island's last elected and thus constitutional leader, he vowed to contest any election through his party, the GULP. In the post-invasion disarray, this promise alarmed US strategists, since they saw in Gairy

Sir Eric Gairy, soon after his return to Grenada in 1984

a corrupt demagogue who was likely to exacerbate unresolved tensions and even precipitate another revolution. This view also reflected US anxiety over the resurgence of the pro-Bishop faction of the NJM who had regrouped in the shape of the Maurice Bishop Patriotic Movement (MBPM), founded by former PRG ministers George Louison and Kendrick Radix in May 1984. Neither of these two political groups was acceptable to the US.

A number of alternatives were available to Washington. One was the conservative GNP which swiftly announced its intention to participate in any elections. Its record of self-interest and incompetence was hardly inspiring, however, and was unlikely to appeal to a politicised, mainly young, electorate. Another was the Grenada Democratic Movement (GDM), a primarily exile-based grouping, led by law lecturer Francis Alexis. The GDM had strong pro-US credentials but little local support. A third was the liberal, social-democratic current, structured around the National Democratic Party (NDP) and led by former NJM supporter and teacher George Brizan. Politically more progressive than the right-wing GDM, the NDP had more backing in Grenada, due in part to Brizan's popularity. Other groups, such as Winston Whyte's Christian Democratic Labour Party (CDLP), were traditional 'one-man' organisations and were to prove to be ephemeral.

The task for the US and these politicians was to close ranks against Gairy and the MBPM. A first attempt took place in April 1984 with the founding of the Team for National Togetherness (TNT), which represented an electoral alliance between the GNP, the GDM and the NDP. Within a month it had collapsed, however, as Brizan objected to GNP leader Herbert Blaize's insistence on the power of individual veto over policy and candidates. A subsequent realignment placed Brizan with Whyte, while Alexis remained with Blaize. As US and local fears mounted over Gairy, another attempt was made in late August to cement an alliance between the centrist parties. At a meeting on Union Island (a dependency of St Vincent) on 26 August, Blaize, Brizan, Alexis and Whyte agreed to merge their parties into the New National Party (NNP). This at last was the political entity that the US could back, and the regional importance of its establishment could be seen in the presence at the Union Island meeting of the right-wing Prime Ministers of Barbados, St Lucia and St Vincent.

By this time, concern over Gairy's possible electoral revival had prompted open threats that the US would remove all economic assistance in the event of a GULP victory. The creation of the NNP was therefore timely, and a month later the Governor-General announced that elections would be held on 3 December 1984. After much delay and uncertainty, the decision to move ahead reflected several developments. One was the US-supported birth of the NNP itself, thereby providing a plausible electoral opponent to the GULP. Another was the widespread feeling that the Interim Advisory Council's temporary nature was discouraging potential US investors and that an elected government would project a more convincing image of stability. Also relevant was regional pressure to end the invasion and interim chapter with all its controversy and embarrassment and to return Grenada to a semblance of constitutional normalcy.

Winston Whyte soon dropped out of the NNP, but the new party survived more or less intact until the election. Behind the facade of unity, however, conflict broke out between the right-wing GDM leaders and Brizan's liberals. Blaize's autocratic style also created difficulties, as did a struggle over who should be deputy leader and who eventually would replace Blaize. The ageing and infirm leader of the coalition was popularly likened to a 'ripe mango', and Brizan and Alexis clearly saw themselves as heirs apparent to his position. In the meantime, Gairy solicited US support by asking in the GULP manifesto for a permanent US military presence and emphasising his commitment to democracy and the private sector. The US embassy furiously denied his claim that he had already obtained such support.

In the NNP the US and its regional allies had created an intrinsically shaky alliance between normally opposed forces who were lumped together simply to exclude Gairy. The GNP, representing the traditional plantocracy and its parochial values was far removed from Alexis's much more aggressive brand of nationalism. Equally, Brizan, with his commitment to certain social reforms and a state role in economic development was viewed as a radical by other NNP leaders. But, in the absence of a better option, the NNP represented an approximation to the right-wing, pro-US, pro-private sector government that Washington wished to see installed in St George's. Looked at positively, it had a blend of experience and enthusiasm; looked at more cynically, it contained an unstable mix of colonial conservatism and anti-communist exile zeal.

Elections 1984

From the outset, many Grenadians were suspicious of the process of voter registration. It was alleged, for instance, that the extensive data provided for inclusion on the electoral list — including photographs and fingerprints — was computerised and sent to Barbados for some unspecified purpose. Later, both the GULP and the MBPM complained that their supporters had experienced problems in registering. The MBPM, in particular, stated that some supporters who had been arrested by the US forces and then released on condition that they did not engage in political activity were deterred from registering. At the end of October, moreover, Sir Paul Scoon sacked Roy Chasteau, the Election Supervisor, seemingly because he had agreed to accept late registrations from such voters. When 21 of Chasteau's staff took industrial action, they were also dismissed. Subsequently, Chasteau made further allegations of irregularities. The final electorate was 48,000, 16,000 fewer than in the previous elections in 1976. The figure was a comment both on voter reluctance in 1984 and Gairy's distortion of figures eight years earlier as well as the perennial process of emigration.

US organisations contributed openly and significantly to the NNP campaign. Two advisors, funded by a direct-mail appeal to wealthy US conservatives, provided technical assistance. The Council for National Policy, a shadowy New Right grouping involving Jerry Falwell, Joseph Coors (of the brewing empire) and Jesse Helms, offered financial support, while former Reagan aide, Morton C. Blackwell (a veteran of the 1984 El Salvador elections) was also involved. Contributors to the NNP included the National Republican Institute for International Affairs and the extreme right-wing 'Accuracy in Media' group. A body known as the Grenada Civic Awareness Organisation, made up of conservative businessmen and church leaders, received money from the US government-funded National Endowment for Democracy and was clearly pro-NNP in bias. AIFLD, too, organised seminars in the weeks preceding voting. The election thus attracted the attention of much of the 'Irangate' network of pro-contra activists. Support was also forthcoming from two regional right-wing parties: Tom Adams's Barbados Labour Party and Edward Seaga's Jamaica Labour Party.

As a result, the NNP was able to engage in a traditional 'rum and corned beef' election campaign. Paying several hundred helpers between US$20 and US$30 a week for six weeks, the NNP distributed teeshirts, pens, notebooks and food baskets, while aircraft were chartered to fly above the island, trailing NNP slogans. On election day itself, taxi drivers were reportedly paid up to US$250 to ferry NNP voters to the polling stations. In contrast, the GULP lost some of its traditional business supporters to the NNP and suffered a drop in financial backing, especially as it became widely known that the US had threatened to suspend aid if Gairy's party won. The MBPM campaigned on a very low budget, while a handful of independents and CDLP candidates gradually faded from view or dropped out altogether.

The voting was a relief to Washington and to the majority of Grenadians who feared the return of Gairy. The NNP took 14 of the island's 15 seats, with approximately 59 per cent of the vote, while the GULP polled 36 per cent and took the single seat of St Andrew's North-East. The MBPM, meanwhile, took 5 per cent of the vote, losing its deposit in 12 of the 13 seats it contested. The figures suggested three facts: that the US initiative in creating and promoting a centrist coalition (although nominally a single party) had succeeded in defeating the GULP; that the GULP and Gairy still commanded significant loyalty and had polled highly throughout the island; and that the MBPM, although drawing big crowds to meetings and rallies, was not yet ready to achieve electoral success because of popular misgivings over recent events. The jailed leaders of the RMC, meanwhile, derided the elections as a rebuff to Gairy, a popular rejection of the MBPM's 'opportunistic' attempt to make capital out of Bishop's death, and a victory for 'imperialism and the bourgeoisie'.

The UN and Commonwealth both declined invitations to send observers to the elections. Independent observers from Britain, Canada and West Germany concluded that they were fair and free, although both the GULP and the MBPM half-heartedly accused the authorities of ballot-rigging.

Once assured of victory, Blaize moved quickly to strengthen the position of his faction within the ruling party. He allotted key cabinet posts to himself (Finance, Trade, Home Affairs, Security) and to GNP loyalists such as Ben Jones (Foreign Affairs), George McGuire (Education) and Danny Williams (Health). Brizan was given Agriculture and Alexis Labour. The other principal GDM activist, Keith Mitchell, took the important portfolio of Minister of Works. Of ten appointed senators, moreover, seven were directly associated with the former GNP, and one, Eric Pierre, the well known associate of AIFLD, was appointed to represent the labour movement with no prior consultation with the TUC. Critics were quick to point out that some of these senators were supposed to be independent appointments. At the same time, speculation grew as to who would replace Blaize if and when his obvious ill health prevented him from working effectively. An eventual power struggle was predicted between Blaize, Brizan and Alexis.

Cuts and Deficits

The NNP government's first official statements at the opening of parliament were a curious blend of welfare reformism and free-market 'Reaganomics'. While pledging to improve and expand infrastructural development, housing, health and education, the government also promised to cut taxation and reduce public sector expenditure. The policy outline also mentioned that the British government would be sending 'a team of organisation and methods consultants for the specific purpose of rationalising the public service'. Other proposals emphasised security and the development of a new constitution (the situation since the invasion had been that PRG legislation had been haphazardly confirmed or annulled according to the needs of the Advisory Council which had also restored the 1974 constitution). The main thrusts of the NNP were therefore the reduction of the public sector, fiscal reform and infrastructural expansion to attract foreign investment. Behind each of these lay the already established priorities of the US embassy and USAID.

The public sector reduction had been started from the beginning of the Advisory Council's period in office, with sweeping redundancies in most areas of state-run activity. The arrival in Grenada in April 1985 of a team from the British management consultancy firm, Peat, Marwick and Mitchell, marked the next stage in the process. By November, Prime Minister Blaize had received a report which described the civil service as highly overstaffed and inefficient, losing up to 160,000 hours per year due to late arrival and early departure of workers. The report also recommended 229 permanent and 445 temporary civil service jobs to be cut. Publication of the recommendations coincided with news in September 1986 that the government's capital budget would have to be cut by EC$10 million (US$3.7 million)[1] due to a shortfall in revenue. The following month, it was announced that staffing levels would be drastically slashed to reduce a 'massive, unsupportable payroll'.

The move brought the government into direct conflict with the public-sector trade unions, which claimed that the government had promised joint consultations before announcing any measures. Hostility mounted further when in December 1986 the government stated that 1,800 out of a total of 3,000 civil service jobs would be cut over an unspecified period. An early retirement scheme proposed a

---

For the sake of consistency, financial data will be given in US$ as opposed to Eastern Caribbean $ (EC$). The EC$ is pegged to the US$ at the rate of 2.70 to 1.

gratuity and pension only for those with more than 16 years' service. Rejecting the offer, the TAWU, the GUT and the Public Workers Union (PWU) accused ministers of being anti-union, while the government insisted that its aim of reducing the monthly wage bill by US$0.48 million could save it from financial collapse.

Most damaging to the government was the widespread claim that it was using the cuts to victimise political opponents. Critics alleged that people promoted during the PRG regime were being singled out for dismissal. As the 'retrenchment' issue became increasingly controversial, three ministers — George Brizan, Francis Alexis and Tillman Thomas — who, in any case, had lost their internal fight against Blaize, resigned, complaining that the government was carrying out massive redundancies with no retraining provision. Brizan then claimed that NNP supporters were being employed to replace those sacked, asserting that the term 'replacement' was more accurate than 'retrenchment'. Other reports confirmed that longstanding GNP loyalists, many of them retired, were being drafted into the civil service. Sensing political disaster, Keith Mitchell announced in April 1987 that the figure of targeted redundancies had been reduced from 1,800 to 500, since 400 civil servants from a readjusted target of 900 had accepted early retirement.

By January 1988 between 500 and 600 civil servants had been sacked, most with little notice or prospects for retraining. Allegations of political victimisation persisted, as in the case of a chief technical officer in the Ministry of Agriculture who was made redundant shortly after declaring his attention to stand as a candidate for George Brizan's breakaway party. In May, too, it was alleged that permanent secretary Osbert Benjamin had been sacked because he had served as a diplomat under the PRG. Furthermore, civil servants were denied their traditional right of appeal to the non-governmental Public Service Commission when provision for appeal against wrongful dismissal was abolished under the 1987 Public Service Reorganisation Act.

For all the government's official statements on the need to trim the civil service, the retrenchment programme was unpopular in most quarters. While USAID officials complained that it had achieved very little in reducing the public-sector payroll, the TUC insisted that it was more of an ideological purge than an effective rationalisation programme. Brizan continued to allege that sackings were politically motivated and pointed to numerous government departments where staffing had increased rather than decreased. By early 1989, the programme had apparently ground to a halt and some retrenchees even returned to better posts, as the NNP government reconsidered the political consequences of raising unemployment any higher.

USAID, meanwhile, signalled its impatience with the non-implementation of the full retrenchment scheme by suspending Structural Adjustment Program payments to the hard-pressed government.

Tax Trauma

In the case of taxation, USAID officials had very clear ideas, wishing to use the island as an experiment in radical change. Their plan included shifting the burden of taxation away from high earners towards sales taxes affecting rich and poor alike. What was not foreseen was the Grenadian Government's inability to collect the new taxes and balance its books.

USAID documents insisted on the need for a 'fiscal (budgetary and tax) reform program' and financial aid was conditional upon its implementation. The budget of April 1985 showed the shape of things to come, as it reduced income tax and increased allowances for higher earners. It also reduced company tax and cut import duties, while looking to increased foreign revenue to fund expenditure. This revenue could only come from the US and other western donors, and it was reported that Blaize had asked Vice-President George Bush for US$200 million in March. The fiscal deficit was put at US$10.4 million. Yet, recognising the contradiction of cutting taxes and expecting higher revenues, Blaize echoed the famous 'voodoo economics' theory of the Reagan administration: 'we are sticking our necks out on the line to prove that you can increase revenue even while you reduce taxes.'

The February 1986 budget was more radical still. Abolishing income tax altogether, it introduced a 20 per cent Value Added Tax (VAT) and a number of new taxes to replace 17 different categories. Again, Blaize forecast a deficit — this time of US$6.6 million — and said that he expected US aid to make up the gap. In October 1985, a US budgetary support grant of US$2.9 million had been approved (bringing total budgetary support to US$12.9 million since January 1984), but USAID documents were now querying how the Grenadian government intended to 'close the still unfinanced $17.3 million gap in its FY85 budget'. Moreover, strong criticism came at once from the Grenada Employers' Federation, the Hotel and Tourism Association and the Chamber of Commerce, who objected not only to VAT but to a new 10 per cent company tax. By July, the situation had become critical, and Blaize was forced to admit that revenue for the first half of 1986 had totalled US$11.42 million, only 29 per cent of the planned annual

US$40 million. In the event, the annual revenue shortfall was US$6.3 million.

The failure was repeated in 1987, when in July Blaize announced a severe cash flow crisis, caused by a continuing shortfall in revenue collection. Again, new taxes were held responsible, notably land transfer tax, property tax and a business levy, introduced in February and reportedly difficult to collect. The three major commodity producer organisations representing cocoa, nutmeg and banana farmers, were more or less refusing to pay the 2.5 per cent levy on gross sales, and even NNP loyalist Norris James, chairman of the Cooperative Nutmeg Association, asserted that the old corporate tax system was much preferable. Complaining that money was urgently needed for severance payments to sacked civil servants, the Prime Minister stated that US$3.3 million was required to avoid financial collapse.

George Brizan underlined the government's crisis in October 1987 when he claimed that VAT revenue was US$1.85 million short of expectation, that the unpopular business levy had generated less than US$0.26 million as opposed to the projected US$1.85 million, and that property transfer tax had brought in less than US$74,000 rather than an anticipated US$2.6 million. Adding that budgetary support from the US was US$5.2 million less than expected, Brizan said that the government had had to take US$2.6 million from the National Insurance Scheme (NIS) simply to pay day-to-day expenses.

In March 1988, Blaize conceded that the government had kept itself afloat during 1987 by borrowing US$7.4 million from the NIS, US$6.9 million from local commercial banks and by receiving US$10 million as a down payment on a 49 per cent shareholding in Grenada Telecommunications Ltd from Cable & Wireless. Scotching rumours that income tax was to be reintroduced, the government increased indirect taxation, bringing in a 10 per cent import surcharge on goods from outside the CARICOM area and adding a 2.5 per cent retailer's margin to the list of price-controlled goods that had hitherto been subject to a VAT rating of 10 per cent or less.

Opposition parties were unanimous in condemning these measures as an attack on the low-paid, while the Chamber of Commerce objected vehemently to the provision that businesses would be taxed at 33 per cent of net profits or 2.5 per cent of gross trading receipts, whichever was the greater. Typical of the business community's objection to the fiscal package were the public remarks of Fred Toppin, chairman and managing director of the import-export company, Jonas Browne and Hubbard. 'The political uncertainties which are plaguing Grenada, as well as the absence of a cohesive and workable taxation policy by government, are proving to be deterrents to the economic growth of the country', he stated. Blaize, by now seemingly oblivious to the business community's disenchantment with government policy, dismissed such objections as 'rantings and ravings'.

The USAID-inspired experiment in fiscal reform had by 1990 saddled the government with a deeply unpopular and seemingly unworkable taxation system which was seen to favour the wealthy few and harm the poor majority. Not that the Chamber of Commerce or the commodity producers associations were enthusiastic about what they saw as unjust levies. The Cooperative Nutmeg Association had resolutely refused to pay the 2.5 per cent levy introduced in 1987 and in January 1989 was threatened with legal action by the government over US$1.85 million in unpaid taxes. The government had also failed to solve its persistent deficit problem; only heavy borrowing and grudging US budgetary support staved off financial collapse. The trade gap was no less disastrous. At the end of 1988 the balance of trade deficit was estimated at US$59.6 million. Credit, too, was tightened, since the government had been forced to empty commercial banks to meet its day-to-day commitments.

The 1989 budget merely shifted the VAT levy from wholesalers and retailers to manufacturers and importers. This was an admission of defeat on the part of the government which had never been able to collect VAT under the preceding tax structure. An Eastern Caribbean Central Bank report revealed that in the first nine months of 1988 revenue collected was only 56 per cent of the annual target and that VAT in particular had produced merely 42 per cent of anticipated annual revenue. Nonetheless, in April 1989 Blaize predicted a surplus on recurrent expenditure for the first time in a decade and publicly thanked God for imbuing him with the 'wisdom to produce for Grenada a balanced budget.' Opposition parties, however, pointed out that the government's record did not inspire confidence and that the poor would lose another two cents in the dollar from increased indirect taxation.

As a consequence of NNP fiscal policy, Grenada's national debt rose steadily from US$59.4 million in 1985 to US$75.9 million in 1986, US$80.85 million in 1987 and US$84.6 million at the end of 1988. Revenue shortfalls in turn led to inability to service the debt and occasional cash-flow crises. In July 1986, for instance, the government had to defer debt repayments of US$4.96 million, including arrears of US$3.25 million on loans from East Germany and Libya contracted by the PRG, while a year later reports emerged that debt servicing payments of US$2.2 million had not been made in the first half of 1987. After the unsuccessful meeting with the IMF in late 1987 Sir Paul Scoon announced that the government would seek to reschedule or refinance a large part of the debt. By then, debt servicing was estimated at almost 42 per cent of the island's Gross Domestic Product.

Dollars Spent (and Misspent)
One of the main thrusts of USAID/NNP policy was to create an environment attractive to foreign investment and tourism through improvements in infrastructure. Emergency road repairs began in November 1983, partly to make good the damage caused by the invasion, while other war-damaged installations such as the Radio Grenada transmitter and the Westerhall telephone exchange were also repaired. By February 1987, USAID claimed to have spent US$11 million on basic infrastructural work. Other major programmes improved tourist facilities (beauty-spots and the Carenage quayside), water supply and electricity.

Some of these programmes were successful and gained support for the NNP government. The electrification programme, in particular, was popular with rural Grenadians, costing an estimated US$1.85 million and bringing electricity to numerous communities. The ambitious and energetic Minister of Public Works, Keith Mitchell, took much of the credit for these advances. Also popular were improvements in water supply (although much of Grenada remains vulnerable to chronic drought) and the 'Special Development Activities' programme which funded small community-based self-help projects on the island. Of the latter USAID remarked that 'this single activity is without doubt the most popular program in the A.I.D. project portfolio.' Equally striking, however, was the resemblance between this low-cost programme — with its emphasis on community involvement in the construction and repair of medical and educational facilities — and the voluntary work programmes of the PRG.

The significant changes brought about by foreign-financed capital investment projects brought with them their own difficulties. One was the problem of running and maintaining expensive infrastructural projects. Soon after it opened, for instance, the international airport was reported to be losing large sums of money. Another was the widespread allegation of corruption against politicians and their associates involved in financial and contractual deals. One allegation centred on the apparent misuse of US$0.74 million of European Community funding for the Eastern Main Road project, while it was also alleged that ministerial and party pressure influenced the selection of workers and advisors for certain public works projects. Further controversy surrounded Keith Mitchell's personal involvement in a private concrete block factory and the government's sale of a burnt-out public building in Grenville to Junior Agriculture Minister Pauline Andrews.

The NNP government never fully shook off the whiff of scandal. A minor crisis occurred in January 1986, when Kenny Lalsingh, a junior Education Minister, resigned, accused of stealing bags of government cement. Other scandals involved allegations of drug-smuggling and bribery at the airport and unsubstantiated but persistent rumours linking senior politicians to cocaine and heroin trafficking. But perhaps the most damaging incident surrounded the collapse of Grenada Airways and the mysterious sale of its single aircraft. Grenada Airways had been set up in mid-1985 as a joint venture between the government and a dubious Miami-based French company, Groupe International de Transport et d'Industrie Petrolière. From the outset, the company which used a single Bandeirante aircraft, acquired from Brazil by the PRG, had a record of incompetence and mismanagement. Plans to build a multi-million dollar hotel complex never materialised, and when the company collapsed, leaving debts of US$1.1 million, it was discovered that the aircraft had been sold to a US company without the government receiving any money. Nor had Brazil been paid for the aircraft, and the government was obliged to pay the Brazilian government, as well as the Grenadian National Commercial Bank the US$0.59 million that it had guaranteed on behalf of Grenada Airways. Attempts by a US loan company to implicate former Aviation Minister, Keith Mitchell, with the missing funds in late 1989 were met with threats of libel suits.

New Alignments, Old Arguments

The unstable NNP government split apart in April 1987, when Francis Alexis, George Brizan and Tillman Thomas resigned their ministerial posts. Factional strife had been evident since mid-1985, when Alexis had staged an abortive internal coup against Blaize, and since then struggles had persisted between Blaize's GNP faction and the currents represented by Alexis and Brizan. With Kenny Lalsingh's sacking another crisis had developed, and any semblance of unity had vanished at the NNP convention in December 1986, when Keith Mitchell had changed factions and masterminded complete GNP control of the NNP. The resigning ministers blamed the retrenchment controversy, the tax reforms and Blaize's 'dictatorial' style. Decisions affecting their ministries were taken, they complained, without any

Prime Minister Herbert Blaize opens the Ramada Renaissance hotel, watched by George Brizan (second right)

consultation, while nepotism was obvious in Blaize's decision to replace the Consul-General in New York with his own daughter.

The split revealed Mitchell's decision to stake his claim to the NNP leadership. It also cemented the recent alliance of Brizan and Alexis — a strange development given the early days of the NNP, when the two politicians had fought for the deputy leadership and Alexis had condemned Brizan as a 'communist'. The alliance was institutionalised three months later with the launch of the National Democratic Congress (NDC), led by Brizan, and comprising not only Alexis and Thomas, but also three other MPs — Lalsingh, Phinsley St Louis (another ex-NNP supporter) and Marcel Peters (who had been the sole GULP MP but had swiftly been expelled by Gairy, taking his seat as an independent). With six parliamentary seats the NDC suddenly represented a credible opposition to the beleaguered NNP.

The formation of the NDC symbolised the final polarisation between the GNP's traditional conservatism and the more dynamic modernising currents of the GDM and NDP. But this latter combination also contained apparent contradictions, between Brizan's liberal reformism and Alexis's right-wing past. Brizan, for instance, openly supported many of the PRG's social programmes, while Alexis was better known for his anti-communism and support for the US development plan. But for both of them, the NNP was clearly a sinking ship, and another imperfect alliance was preferable to political oblivion.

The NDC offered the US an alternative to the NNP, even if it was an open secret that Washington distrusted Brizan for his former NJM links. A policy statement, published in October 1987, emphasised the NDC's commitment to private-sector development (while allowing a role for the state), and pointedly stressed 'the special friendship we have been enjoying with our traditional friends and allies...especially in the light of our experiences in October 1983.' The next stage in wooing US support came in late 1988, when Nicholas Brathwaite, former Chairman of the Interim Advisory Council, was offered the leadership of the party and NDC candidature in Blaize's Carriacou seat. With this move, approved at the January 1989 NDC Convention, a more obviously conservative frontman was put in place in time for the elections constitutionally due by March 1990.

The NNP government, meanwhile, having survived the April 1987 crisis, continued to project itself as Washington's first choice. However, Blaize was becoming increasingly ill as well as unpopular among NNP supporters. After a series of rumours, Keith Mitchell made his bid for leadership in January 1989, unseating Blaize as party chief and outflanking Ben Jones, the representative of the traditional GNP. With Mitchell in control, the NNP could present a rejuvenated and more dynamic image, both to the US and the Grenadian people. This image, however, was obtained at the cost of festering internal disputes between cabinet members. In the months preceding the anticipated elections, the party had in fact split from the government, with open enmity between Blaize and Mitchell. Attempts at mediation by local right-wing leaders of the US-sponsored Caribbean Democratic Union (CDU) could not mend the fractured NNP, which had finally rid itself of the old-fashioned GNP influence in favour of Mitchell's more populist stance.

Other political forces could not be discounted. Gairy's GULP continued to alarm the US with its apparent popularity. After announcing his retirement from politics in late 1987, Gairy purged two potential successors to the leadership in a sudden change of heart, accusing Raphael Fletcher of suspicious links with Libya (he had taught there between 1981 and 1984) and Jerry Seales of breaching party discipline. His eccentricity in no way diminished, Gairy continued to mix crude anti-communism and populism, and was reelected party leader in December 1988. Like the NNP and the NDC,

Gairy tried to court the US, stating that he would offer Washington a permanent military base if elected to power.

On the left, the MBPM also revitalised its image, when Terence Marryshow, a Cuban-trained doctor, replaced Kendrick Radix as leader. The party had already been gathering more support after the 1984 electoral setback and held a number of well attended meetings and conventions. It claimed, with ample justification, to be harassed by the NNP government (see p.107), while it also remains bitterly at odds with the imprisoned leaders of the NJM. They, in turn, are dismissive of the MBPM and claim to represent the authentic legacy of the revolution, even if the NJM does not function in any visible way inside Grenada.

The Bitter End

The dispute over the leadership of the NNP finally came to a head in July 1989 when Blaize sacked Keith Mitchell as a government minister. At the same time, he announced that a commission of inquiry would investigate alleged improprieties and misappropriation of funds in five government departments and four statutory bodies, all falling under Mitchell's various ministries. A day later, Blaize stated that he had formed a new political party, the National Party, but five days later withdrew the statement, claiming that the new organisation was merely a faction within the existing NNP. With the NNP and ministers in disarray, Mitchell retaliated by attempting to table a motion of no confidence in the government, but the NDC declined to support the motion. In the event, the opposition MPs were given no chance to unseat Blaize, as the Prime Minister prorogued (or suspended) parliament on 23 August, thereby avoiding any no confidence vote and putting off the need to call a general election.

Blaize's delaying tactic was clearly intended to give him time to form his new political party which was formally launched in September. In reality nothing more than a resurrection of the old GNP, the National Party (TNP) had Ben Jones as deputy leader and George McGuire as chairman, both of whom were Blaize loyalists. The creation of the TNP did nothing to offset the sense of limbo that had overtaken Grenadian politics since the collapse of the NNP government and the suspension of parliament. Blaize stubbornly refused to call elections, ignoring public opinion and persevering in what had become an untenable political situation.

As his health deteriorated, the Prime Minister was trapped in a final crisis which typified the failings of the previous five years. As 7,000

Main Political Parties, Leaders and Coalitions since the invasion

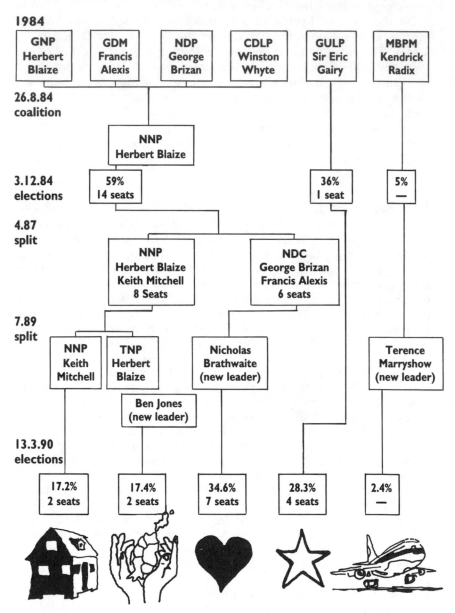

1984

| GNP Herbert Blaize | GDM Francis Alexis | NDP George Brizan | CDLP Winston Whyte | GULP Sir Eric Gairy | MBPM Kendrick Radix |

26.8.84 coalition

NNP Herbert Blaize

3.12.84 elections

59% 14 seats   36% 1 seat   5% —

4.87 split

NNP Herbert Blaize Keith Mitchell 8 Seats

NDC George Brizan Francis Alexis 6 seats

7.89 split

NNP Keith Mitchell

TNP Herbert Blaize

Nicholas Brathwaite (new leader)

Terence Marryshow (new leader)

Ben Jones (new leader)

13.3.90 elections

17.2% 2 seats   17.4% 2 seats   34.6% 7 seats   28.3% 4 seats   2.4% —

public sector workers went on strike at the beginning of December 1989 calling for US$9.25 million in back pay for the period 1987-9, Blaize unsuccessfully appealed to Britain and the US for loans. Faced with mounting industrial action, he was forced to recall parliament on 14 December to obtain approval for government borrowing of US$11 million. Despite gaining approval, Blaize announced the following day that the government had raised US$6.5 million by selling a further 21 per cent shareholding in Grenada Telecommunications Ltd to Cable & Wireless, thereby giving the British company a 70 per cent stake in the formerly state-owned enterprise. Not only was the divestment decision not debated in parliament, but it was also clearly aimed at solving a short-term problem at the expense of long-term national interests.

Four days after his controversial announcement, Herbert Blaize died of cancer, to be succeeded as Prime Minister and leader of the TNP by his long-time deputy, Ben Jones. Blaize's death further emphasised the government's loss of legitimacy and presented Jones with the unavoidable task of calling elections which were constitutionally due by 28 March 1990. On 10 February, after further procrastinations, Jones set the date for 13 March — eleven years to the day since the overthrow of Gairy and the arrival in power of the PRG.

Elections 1990

From the start of the month-long electoral campaign, it was clear that no one political party could claim a commanding lead. The original NNP coalition of 1984 had by now broken into three mutually antagonistic parties — Brathwaite's NDC, Jones's TNP and Mitchell's NNP — while Gairy's GULP was still a force to be reckoned with. Although all the main parties spoke confidently of winning an overall majority, speculation persisted as to the possibility of alliances and coalitions in the event of an inconclusive result in voting for the 15-seat parliament. Two possibilities seemed more plausible than the others: an eventual agreement between the NDC and the TNP, both parties representing middle-class and urban voters; or an alliance between the GULP and the NDC, based on a common appeal to the poorer rural sectors of the population.

Even before the collapse of the Blaize government, a conspicuous rapprochement between Mitchell and Gairy had been taking place. Some of Mitchell's speeches in 1989 had resembled the vintage Gairyism of the 1950s, with their appeal to the poor and marginalised.

In May of that year, for instance, he had spoken of his struggle against the political elite:

> There are those inside the NNP and those outside the NNP, who will never accept Keith Mitchell as leader because Keith Mitchell is supposed to be a little black boy from Happy Hill [a village on the island's west coast] who used to wear patched pants and walk bare feet. I've heard all those comments of a little black boy and patched pants and bare feet... but I'm proud of being a little black boy because I believe that all of us in Grenada are little black boys ready for justice in this beautiful country.

In contrast to Mitchell's populism, the NDC projected an image of technocratic competence, emphasising Brathwaite's role in the Interim Advisory Council and the leadership qualities of George Brizan and Francis Alexis. The party's manifesto promised an overhaul of the NNP government's disastrous fiscal policy and increased commitment towards social programmes. But, in many respects, the parties' manifestos provided few significant variations in ideological perspective. All looked to export-based agriculture, manufacturing, tourism and foreign investment as the key to Grenada's development. Only the MBPM offered a radical alternative, promising a return to many of the social policies of the PRG, an emphasis on state planning and revitalising the cooperative sector.

The election, for the most part, was less centred on policies than on personalities. Prominent among these was Eric Gairy, who campaigned with a typically eccentric mixture of religious mysticism and personality cult. He insisted that the 13 March date was part of a cosmic scheme to return him to power and held meetings which consisted more of hymn singing than political speeches. Keith Mitchell also attempted to emphasise his own personal following and made much of his reputation for efficiency and dynamism. With Nicholas Brathwaite mostly in Carriacou, the NDC deputy leaders, George Brizan and Francis Alexis, took a higher profile than the party leader. Ben Jones, meanwhile, ran a lacklustre campaign for the ruling TNP.

Accusations and allegations abounded. Jones's television broadcast dwelled on the violence of the Gairy era and appealed to the electorate to vote for moderation. Gairy, in return, accused the NDC of intimidating and beating up his supporters. The NDC concentrated on vilifying Keith Mitchell, accusing him of criminal activity and one of his candidates, Winston Whyte, of having been instrumental in setting up the Mongoose Gang during the Gairy regime. There was ample evidence of 'dirty tricks', notably against the GULP. An anonymous poster was circulated, linking Gairy with Jim Jones of the

Guyana mass suicide notoriety. Finally, a forged airline ticket was circulated, purportedly showing that Gairy intended to leave the island on the day of the election for health reasons.

The US adopted an official position of impartiality, unlike in 1984. However, the Republican-financed Caribbean Democratic Union (CDU) was active in support of Mitchell's NNP, and on the eve of polling Prime Minister Jones warned that militants from the CDU-affiliated Jamaica Labour Party were intending to disrupt the elections with violence. Other allegations connected US financial sources with the campaign to discredit Gairy. In the event, the US presence, both political and military, was extremely low key, reflecting Washington's loss of interest in Grenada.

Coalition Again

The results confirmed what opinion polls and forecasts had predicted. A low turn out of 65 per cent of voters gave no party an overall majority and forced an immediate round of political dealing. With seven out of a total of 15 seats, and 34 per cent of the vote, the NDC was unable to form a government without support from another party or individual. Gairy's GULP took four seats (three more than in 1984) but with a reduced percentage share of 28 per cent. The TNP and the NNP won 2 seats each (with 17 per cent of the vote each), while the MBPM gained only 2.4 per cent of the votes. The main surprise was perhaps the poor showing of Mitchell's NNP which some commentators had expected to capture up to six seats.

In the ensuing stalemate everything depended on the position of Jones's TNP, since an agreement between the NDC and either Gairy or Mitchell was unthinkable. A coalition between the NDC and the TNP at first seemed assured, but within a day of the inconclusive results another possibility had emerged: that Gairy, Mitchell and Jones would form an alternative coalition. According to the Caribbean News agency (CANA), Jones was on the point of accepting Gairy's offer to retain the prime ministership before a public message from his constituency members reminded him that he had spent his career opposing Gairy and that an agreement 'with bad men' would not be acceptable to the party. The prospect of Gairy regaining political influence (although he had narrowly failed to win his traditional St George's South seat) had briefly caused alarm among many sectors of Grenadian society, as people feared retribution against those associated with the revolutionary period.

Philip Wolmuth

Nicholas Brathwaite, 1984

The immediate crisis was temporarily resolved when Sir Paul Scoon invited Nicholas Brathwaite to form the next government, thereby removing the growing possibility of new elections. After some delays, Ben Jones agreed that he and fellow TNP MP, Alleyne Walker, would join the government; they were also joined by a GULP dissident, Edzel Thomas.

With the addition of three other MPs, the NDC could claim a majority of 10 out of 15 seats. This majority, however, was in reality even more fragile than that of the preceding NNP government. Not only was it based on a purely pragmatic arrangement between the NDC and Jones (who was aware that the TNP would probably be further damaged by fresh elections), but the NDC itself also remained an unstable entity, made up of widely differing political perspectives. The addition of a former GULP candidate made the coalition even more lacking in clear political outlook. It remained a question of time before differences emerged within the new government.

Nevertheless, posts were distributed according to the deal struck: Jones became Minister of Agriculture and Walker and Thomas took junior appointments. Brathwaite became not only Prime Minister, but also Minister of External Affairs, Minister of Home Affairs, Minister of National Security and Minister for Carriacou and Petit Martinique Affairs. To George Brizan went Finance, Trade and Industry, and to Francis Alexis the post of Attorney-General and Minister of Legal Affairs and Local Government.

A New Beginning?

Eleven years after the coup which ousted Eric Gairy, the veteran politician came close to regaining political power in what was almost certainly his last election. Gairy himself failed to retake his seat by a small margin, and another GULP candidate trailed the winning NDC candidate by only 17 votes. The GULP won only four out of fifteen seats, yet came second in a further ten constituencies. Gairyism, as an electoral force, was far from routed and indeed came very close to holding the balance of power after the 1990 elections.

The resilience of Gairy's popularity was partly a symptom of entrenched loyalties among a declining generation of Grenadian voters. But it was also further evidence of a political vacuum which no post-revolutionary party or leader has been able to fill. Since October 1983 Grenada's politics have been dominated by a series of tactical and often opportunistic alliances, of which the NDC-led government is another example. Identifiable policies and principles have come a poor second to pragmatic deals in which politicians abandon their parties and programmes in order to obtain or hold on to power. In this context, Gairyism at least offers continuity. While there is considerable popular distrust of the demagoguery associated with Gairy, there is also widespread aversion to what is seen as cynical 'backroom' politics.

Grenada's continuing political vacuum presents a serious challenge to the island's government which must contend with deepening scepticism and disillusionment, particularly among the young. It also acts as an obstacle to the USAID-designed development strategy which lays great emphasis on political stability and efficient government, neither of which are guaranteed by coalition rule. Most importantly, it means that the tensions and trauma surrounding Grenada's recent history remain largely unresolved through a new political direction. To that extent, Grenada gives the impression of being caught in the past, unable to shake off fully the influence of the two men who dominated its post-independence development — Eric Gairy and Maurice Bishop.

Chapter 3
Harsh Medicine

'Grenada's recent economic achievement makes it the envy of developing countries.'
Prime Minister Blaize, Budget speech 1988.

'Never before in the last twenty-five years has Grenada's economy been so badly managed as it is today.'
NDC opposition party leaflet, October 1987.

Although rich in agricultural resources, Grenada has always been a poor country for the great majority of its inhabitants. Under the colonial system, the island shipped its bananas, sugar and spices over to Britain. As British influence in the Caribbean faded, the US took over, and Grenada slipped into a neo-colonial state of dependency, where foreign companies, a plantocracy and a tiny local elite made profits out of a restricted range of export crops and trading. Under both systems, Grenada sold cheap and bought dear, and what wealth stayed in the island remained in few hands. A state sector (comprising social services, statutory export boards and public facilities) also existed and during the Gairy regime served often to reward party loyalists, punish opponents and further the interests of a small urban middle class. Up until the mid-1970s, the majority of Grenadians experienced levels of deprivation and exclusion that had not drastically changed since the beginning of the 20th century.

After taking power in 1979, the PRG was thus faced with overwhelming structural economic problems of dependency and underdevelopment. Its attempts to address these problems and to create new participatory structures through trade unions, women's organisations and local government bodies were judged by the Reagan administration as politically unorthodox and suspect. At the same time, the US also viewed the PRG's economic development programme as inefficient and repressive. In particular, it condemned the PRG's 'statism', its emphasis on the role of the state in a mixed economy, as a disincentive to growth and prosperity. The PRG's sin in US eyes was above all a question of foreign policy: it was openly friendly with Cuba, conspicuously took part in the international non-aligned movement and forged links with countries such as Libya. But the fact that the PRG publicly rejected capitalism as the only appropriate framework for national development was a further thorn in Washington's flesh and another reason for distrust and hostility.

If the invasion was primarily intended to assert US dominance in the Caribbean, it also offered US policy-makers and technocrats an opportunity to roll back 'statism' and to preach the gospel of private enterprise. This was clearly an attractive proposition for Grenada's business class which enthusiastically spread the message that a new era of prosperity was at hand. For the great majority of Grenadians, however, who had grown accustomed to improved social services and a better quality of life, the prospect of unbridled 'Reaganomics' was less tempting.

The period that has followed the invasion has been one of dramatic economic and social change, introduced nominally by the Interim Advisory Council and then the elected NNP government, but engineered predominantly by USAID and its associates. This change has affected every major aspect of the economy — agriculture, manufacturing, tourism — and the entire structure of social services and welfare. In the name of economic 'freedom', Grenada has been prescribed a particularly strong dose of US-approved privatisation and deregulation. For many, the cure has been far worse than the supposed illness.

Agriculture: The End of an Experiment

Grenada is an overwhelmingly agricultural country, where natural fertility is counterbalanced by a shortage of prime land. Much of the best arable land in flat areas belongs to large privately-owned estates or the government, and of this a high percentage is under-used or idle. In contrast, an estimated 36 per cent of the population lives directly from farming smallholdings of 4 acres or less. In many cases, small-scale agriculture is little more than 'backyard farming', where a family may grow bananas, mangoes and 'ground provisions' (yams, dasheens and other root crops) to supplement its diet and income.

Recent figures suggest that approximately 7,000 farmers produce cocoa, 7,000 nutmeg, 1,400 bananas, 400 sugar-cane and 600 vegetables. With an estimated 4,000 additional agricultural and related workers, official statistics show that more than half of the population is partly or fully dependent on agriculture for its livelihood. Within this sector, many people work smallholdings with family labour and may also be employed irregularly by larger landowners on an informal basis. In 1986, agriculture accounted for 25 per cent of GDP and 70 per cent of exports, totalling US$21.8 million in value.

When the PRG took power, it discovered that a third of Grenada's arable land was uncultivated and that much of this belonged to absentee land-owners. Rejecting collectivisation as an immediate option, the PRG undertook a gradual land reform, taking unused land into state control on fixed-term leases for the development of the state and cooperative sectors. It also inherited some 25 estates expropriated by Gairy, totalling approximately 4,000 acres. Additional state acquisitions took the total to over 8,000 acres, or about 20 per cent of the island's arable land.

The Grenada Farms Corporation (GFC) was set up in 1980 to administer the state sector and had several aims. Firstly, it enabled the government to play a role in rationalising and modernising traditional agricultural exports which had declined under the indifference and incompetence of the Gairy regime. Secondly, it experimented with diversification as a way out of Grenada's dependency on this small range of exports. Thirdly, it tried to improve the lot of Grenada's 'agro-proletariat' — the poorest sector of the rural population — by bringing some estate-workers into the state sector with guaranteed minimum wage levels, sick pay, pensions and other benefits. Almost 1,000 GFC employees were entitled to improved conditions, including maternity leave and health care visits under the State Farms Health Programme.

The PRG also gave assistance to private farmers through the framework of the Productive Farmers' Union (PFU) with an emphasis on technical advice, credit and training. Assistance was also given with marketing by the Marketing and National Import Board (MNIB) which tried to encourage diversification by finding new markets for alternative products. The PRG was also keen to add value to agricultural produce through an agro-processing industry, and built the 'Spice Isle' plant which processed juices, jams and nectars for export and domestic consumption. Ambitious plans for increased diversification won the support of international agencies, and in 1983, the PRG successfully negotiated a US$7.8 million loan from the World Bank to support its agricultural programme.

In terms of exports, however, the PRG brought about little change, and Grenada remained dependent upon its three traditional crops: cocoa, nutmeg (and mace) and bananas. In the case of cocoa and nutmeg, whose origins lay in mid-19th century peasant production, the PRG sought to improve production and consolidate new markets. The Canadian International Development Agency (CIDA) offered US$6 million in 1981 to finance a cocoa rehabilitation project, which was intended to renew ageing plantations and modernise technology. At the same time, the PRG initiated discussions with the Indonesian government to create a nutmeg producers' cartel (Indonesia producing 75 per cent of the world's total and Grenada 25 per cent). Grenada signed an agreement to export nutmeg to the USSR, but only the first year of the contract took place before the invasion cut it short. The PRG also held exploratory talks with other potential banana importers but achieved no actual orders.

During the PRG years, the export staples also suffered badly due to factors beyond the government's control. The hurricanes of 1979 and 1980 destroyed 40 per cent of banana production, 27 per cent of nutmeg trees and 19 per cent of the cocoa crop. This had a long-term effect, since tree crops such as nutmeg and cocoa take several years to mature. The depreciation of the pound's value against the US dollar also hit agriculture badly, since some cocoa and all bananas were paid for in sterling, while inputs such as fertilisers and pesticides often had to be purchased with dollars. Market prices were also unpredictable; in 1980, the international prices of nutmeg, cocoa and bananas fell by an average of 22 per cent.

PRG agricultural policy was by no means an unqualified success. The GFC, in particular, had a poor productivity record, while the cooperative sector also failed to match expectations. But improvements in feeder roads, the agro-processing initiative and increased domestic production all moved the country in the direction of increased self-sufficiency (food as a percentage of imports dropped from 30.6 per cent to 27.5 per cent between 1979 and 1982) and diversification.

The invasion signalled the end of the experiment and a shift towards private sector-led agricultural development. In the initial onslaught on state-run organisations, several training and research organisations were either destroyed, downgraded or abandoned. The dismantling of the GFC meant that considerable investment was wasted, as in the case of Belvedere Farm which had been transformed from virtual disuse into the island's second largest banana farm with a PRG investment of US$120,000. Belvedere was returned to its owner who did nothing with the estate, and ironically the government was later forced to repurchase 200 acres for distribution to small farmers and estate workers.

The breaking up of the GFC led to the 'model farms' project. Initially, USAID had hoped that private farmers would eagerly reclaim or buy the divested state farms, but few had taken up the opportunity. As a 'second-best' option the model farms scheme sought to increase the number of private smallholders by creating what USAID described as 'viable, privately-held family farms'. A few lots of 15 acres were distributed on long leases, while more of 7 acres or one-half acre were handed out from otherwise abandoned estates or former state farms. Much of the land remained in government hands, the GFC being renamed the Grenada Model Farms Corporation. The government was also intended to provide support in the form of infrastructural improvement, credit and subsidies.

The initial impetus of the scheme, championed by Agriculture Minister George Brizan, was not sustained, however, as US and government funding dwindled. Of US$1.6 million earmarked by the government for expenditure on the model farms in the 1987 budget, only US$198,000 was actually spent. Much of USAID's US$1.7 million budget, meanwhile, was swallowed up by consultancies, surveys and training, while European Community aid remained relatively small. By 1989, the programme was more or less inactive, and some model farms had already been abandoned as economically unviable. With only some 60 actually in operation, totalling 500 out of a projected 3,400 acres, the scheme had a minimal impact on unemployment.

Model farms were intended to produce new agricultural exports, together with traditional crops. The USAID-funded regional High Impact Agricultural Marketing and Production Programme (HIAMP) encourages Grenadian farmers to export vegetables such as breadfruit and sweet potatoes as well as flowers and spices to the US market. Individual initiatives have included seamoss and paw-paw production, while larger estates have exported rum to the US market.

Such production, however, remains insignificant when compared to the three traditional export crops: nutmeg, cocoa and bananas. Here, in contrast to the PRG, the NNP government was fortunate in terms of weather and world prices. The marketing agreement over nutmeg was finally signed with Indonesia in April 1987, and after several years of depressed prices the Grenada Cooperative Nutmeg Association reported 1987 earnings of US$9.5 million and US$13 million in 1988. Bananas, too, have been more profitable, especially since the pound's rise against the dollar in 1987. Production levels have remained at about 8 or 9,000 tons annually, but the US$4.4 million earned by farmers in 1988 was US$0.74 million more than the previous year.

Cocoa, meanwhile, received the large amounts of Canadian aid negotiated by the PRG, and farmers received substantial subsidies in the form of above-market price advance payments, even if the government attempted to impose its unpopular 2.5 per cent levy on commodity producer organisations.

The agricultural sector generated considerable income through a combination of high world prices and foreign assistance. The government also benefited from infrastructural programmes, notably rural feeder roads, developed or started by the PRG. Some of its schemes, such as the opening of a privately-run agro-processing plant also resembled PRG policy, even if the emphasis was very much on private entrepreneurship. The government broke up large publicly owned farms, replacing them with tiny, family operated smallholdings in which organised labour is no longer feasible.

Yet the structural problems of vulnerability to fluctuations in market prices and dependency on foreign markets that the PRG was attempting to address remain ignored. Increasingly violent hurricanes and unpredictable weather conditions also pose a permanent threat, even if the hurricanes and droughts of 1988 and 1989 did not affect Grenada. More worrying still is the future of the banana industry once

Philip Wolmuth

Grading mace at the Gouyave Nutmeg Station.

the single European market comes into operation in 1992. This will possibly abolish the preferential treatment that Grenada and the other Windward producers enjoy within the British market. Geest plc, the British-based transnational that has had a monopoly over banana exports since 1954, has diversified increasingly into food processing and has made it clear that it will work according to market logic if the preferential status is abolished. Grenada's other exports — nutmeg and cocoa — are also subject to the vagaries of world markets and demand. The high prices paid for nutmeg are encouraging increased production, but this goes against the trading agreement with Indonesia which limits each country's output. This agreement, moreover, briefly appeared threatened in 1989 by Grenadian allegations that Indonesia had exceeded its quota, but the agreement was eventually restored.

The combination of windfall earnings, 'mini-booms' and market-oriented development has not only discouraged diversification and domestic food production, but has also done nothing for the poorest sectors of the rural population. As a result of the GMMIWU-led strike, estate workers received a wage rise in 1986 which took the male daily rate to EC$13 and the female rate to EC$12.50 (approximately US$5 per day), and these rates are theoretically enforced by the Ministry of Labour. But the general trend is away from estate agriculture towards smaller productive units which depend upon family labour and occasional casual employment. Here, wages cannot be properly monitored, and informal arrangements often exist between members of a gīven community. The wealth generated by high nutmeg and banana prices is therefore not fairly distributed, while ever increasing amounts of land fall into under-use despite the model farms scheme.

Fishing, meanwhile, has undergone a parallel shift from state-led investment to the private sector with a similar emphasis on small-scale enterprise. Under the PRG, a National Fishing Corporation had been established with Cuban assistance with the aim of creating a state-run fleet of 20 trawlers. Despite major problems with boat engines and wildly optimistic production targets, the state sector did manage to set up a fish-processing factory which made Grenada self-sufficient in the popular staple of salted fish as well as an exporter within the region. The PRG encouraged the private sector, introducing training in new methods. It also provided credit, boats and cold storage facilities, and improved fish-markets opened in Gouyave and Sauteurs. With funding from the UN's International Fund for Agricultural Development (IFAD), this modernisation programme was intended to link up with the traditional industry of boat-building on the island of Carriacou.

The NNP government inherited the IFAD scheme and opened a cold storage facility and retail outlet in St George's in 1988. The Cuban trawlers, however, were virtually given away to private fishermen at prices below what had recently been spent by the PRG on upgrading the engines. Even more controversial was the decision to grant licences to foreign trawlers to fish in Grenadian waters. These boats, mainly from the US, fish for swordfish, a species already over-fished to the brink of extinction. In the meantime, fishing has largely returned to its traditional small-scale units, with drastically reduced government investment.

Manufacturing, Tourism and Growth

In its mixed economy development model, the PRG was anxious to encourage local private-sector investment while minimising the exploitative influence of transnationals. Despite the private sector's suspicions of the PRG, certain areas of private manufacturing experienced growth and profitability between 1980 and 1983. With the benefit of tax concessions, credit facilities, the removal of Gairy's corruption and the effective prohibition of transnational competition, Grenadian and regional entrepreneurs were involved in furniture manufacturing, brewing and distilling, soft drinks, poultry feed, coconut oil, flour and wheat products and textiles. The two latter sectors registered profit rises of 7.8 per cent and 10.6 per cent respectively between 1981 and 1982.

Other manufacturing was state-led, and successes included Grenada Agro-Industries, the 'Sandino' construction plant, the state-owned Grenada Sugar Company (which produces rum and almost broke even for the first time in many years) and the Coffee Processing Plant. Grencraft, the marketing branch of the Grenada National Institute of Handicraft, was instrumental in creating cottage-industries and exported goods to other Caribbean territories. Between 1981 and 1982, the state sector, including farms, hotels, agro-industrial plants, transport, electricity, telecommunications and banks, grew in gross production by 34 per cent.

A construction boom fuelled growth under the PRG. The international airport, in particular, supported by US$60 million worth of direct Cuban assistance, generated 250 jobs, while road building and state-sector construction in low-cost housing, medical and educational facilities stimulated employment and construction-related production. State-owned quarries, asphalt plants and machinery pools all contributed to growth. The PRG's overall capital spending between

1980 and 1982 came to US$81.7 million, dwarfing the US$3 million in Gairy's 1978 budget.

The PRG saw the airport as the linchpin of a diversified economy, in which tourism would play a major part. It overcame its political misgivings over the traditionally negative impact of tourism — the creation of enclaves, the predominance of transnationals, the devaluation of cultural traditions — and championed a 'new tourism', concentrating on new markets and new linkages between the industry and other economic sectors. The new markets, including visitors from other Caribbean territories and non-high income tourists from the US and Canada, failed, however, to compensate for the drop in quantity and spending-power of the traditional tourist markets despite vigorous promotion in the US and Europe. This was in part due to US propaganda against revolutionary Grenada, including negative press coverage about the island. Other factors were recession in the US and Europe and the sheer difficulty of reaching the island until the airport was finished. As a result, stopover tourist arrivals declined from 32,000 in 1978 to 23,000 in 1982, while cruise ship visits became much less frequent.

The PRG's overall approach, combining extensive capital investment, small-scale manufacturing, tourism and agriculture, was not merely successful in winning the support of most Grenadians, but even drew praise from the World Bank. A 1982 memorandum stated:

> The `government which came to power in 1979 inherited a deteriorating economy, and is now addressing the task of rehabilitation and of laying better foundations for growth within the framework of a mixed economy... Government objectives are centered on the critical development issues and touch on the country's most promising development areas.

While characterised as a hard-line Marxist by US propagandists, Finance Minister Bernard Coard earned a reputation as a shrewd financial manager, obtaining loans and grants on excellent conditions, holding down the national debt and controlling government expenditure. An IMF report of 1983 noted that inflation was well under control due to improvements in domestic food supplies. The PRG claimed a steady growth rate, rising from minus 3.2 per cent in 1978 to 5.5 per cent in 1982. These figures, however, were later disputed by the Interim Advisory Council, which estimated overall growth over 1978-82 at 0.2 per cent. This estimate was again revised in the 1984 budget to give average annual growth over 1979-82 of 3 per cent, followed by minus 2 per cent in 1983.

In contrast to the PRG, the post-invasion administrations have pinned their hopes on foreign capital as the source of economic growth. This capital has failed to materialise sufficiently to bring about the anticipated boom in manufacturing, even if growth, as elsewhere in the Eastern Caribbean, has been strong. Growth in this sector reached 16 per cent in 1987, according to USAID, but this followed a poor showing in 1986 and fell to 10.3 per cent in 1988. But despite impressive growth figures, manufacturing remains a small part of Grenada's economy and as a percentage share of GDP is relatively the smallest among the OECS countries. Nor is manufacturing in Grenada technologically advanced; the leading contributors to the 1988 growth in output were soft drinks, rum and retread tyres.

Those companies that have arrived benefit from the generous conditions of the government's investment code as well as from the incentives available to US firms under the Caribbean Basin Initiative. An investment treaty signed with the US in 1986 gave US companies equal tax treatment with their Grenadian counterparts and provided for exchange-control-free repatriation of funds. Even these inducements, however, have failed to attract more than a handful of US companies, all of which are involved in low-wage assembly work and textiles. Other manufacturing revolves around agro-exports such as rum, coconut oil, lime juice, honey and spices, taking place in small and rudimentary plants.

According to the TUC, union activity is strongly discouraged in the new factories at the Frequente industrial estate. One senior TUC official alleges that workers have been dismissed for attempting to organise unions inside the factories, where wages average approximately EC$300 (US$110) per month for the largely female workforce. North American companies who have won USAID contracts for road-building and other infrastructural development are also anti-union. Even so, work on the road-building projects has been much sought after, particularly by agricultural labourers before their 1986 pay increase. Critics of the government allege that employment on the Eastern Main Road scheme was often reserved for NNP supporters and that the slow progress made on the scheme does not account for apparently missing funds.

Tourism is the second principal element in current economic thinking. In this sector, growth has been dramatic, and in 1988 record receipts of US$28.2 million were registered from a 7.6 per cent annual increase in visitors. Several new, refurbished and expanded hotels are expected to expand the island's tourist capability, increasing room capacity from 850 to 1,040. An announcement in May 1989 that American Airlines would be bringing approximately 50,000 passengers to Grenada annually, prompted a government claim that another 500 hotel rooms could be constructed within six months. Over 135,000 of the approximately 200,000 tourists in 1988, however, were cruise ship visitors, spending limited time and money in the capital alone. There is little 'trickle down' of tourist sector income into the economy as a whole, apart from consumption of locally grown produce and handicraft.

The linkages between the tourist and agricultural sectors, encouraged by the PRG, have partly survived, according to a former Tourism Director, even though the current emphasis is very much upon the luxury end of the tourist market. A repeated complaint among hoteliers was that the NNP government failed to promote the island internationally. They also complained that the tourism budget was smaller than it was under the PRG. As a result, the sector remains unplanned, leaving individual hoteliers to organise their own advertising. American Airlines, in announcing its decision to fly to Grenada, reportedly demanded that the government spend at least US$200,000 in promoting the island in the US travel market. On top of this, Grenada still suffers from an image problem in the US, where potential visitors are deterred by the belief that Grenada is still a trouble spot.

In tourism much of the growth is attributable to local and regional entrepreneurs rather than foreign investors. The large hotel companies have not arrived in Grenada, despite the government's generous incentives, while local investors have opened small and medium-sized hotels and guesthouses. Equally, in manufacturing and commerce, the great majority of investment comes from Grenadians, Trinidadians and other Caribbean entrepreneurs. To this must be added the economic stimulus of remittances sent from Grenadians abroad to relatives (conservatively estimated at US$5 million per year) and the steady influx of Grenadians who return to the island after working abroad to retire or invest. Most rural villages contain at least one large and modern house belonging to a returned Grenadian, and the money invested in construction, business and agriculture is of major importance to the economy. In the view of an USAID economist, much of Grenada's recent economic growth (5.6 per cent, 6 per cent and 5.3 per cent in 1986, 1987 and 1988 respectively) can be attributed to small local investors.

Unemployment

The growth in certain sectors of the economy and a series of export 'mini-booms' have not prevented a huge rise in recorded unemployment since October 1983 due to the disbanding of the PRA, the dismantling of the public and cooperative sectors and the sacking of PRG supporters in the civil service. Job losses have been most acute in areas such as state farms (1,000), farm road construction (300), the Youth Employment Project and state-run enterprises such as quarries, construction and agro-industry. During the NNP government, moreover, the trend towards public sector reductions resulted in the retrenchment scheme and the loss of an estimated 600 jobs. Many sacked civil servants were left in desperate straits, since according to a TAWU official in June 1988, no severance pay had been forthcoming to individuals dismissed since May 1986. By mid-1984, unemployment had risen from the PRG estimate of 14 per cent to at least 30 per cent. CDB and USAID figures and unofficial estimates (no official government figures are available) have since put the figure at over 30 per cent, while TUC officials argue that it is nearer 40 per cent, approaching the 49 per cent which, the PRG claimed, existed during the Gairy government.

The NNP government firstly contested the figures issued by the PRG in 1982, and claimed that they were distorted by expanded

Poor rural housing

Jim Rudin

membership of the armed forces and labour-intensive infrastructural work such as the airport construction. It did not, however, recognise that these objections might apply also to its own security services and infrastructural schemes. It also claimed in each budget speech that foreign investment was creating jobs and that unemployment was declining. In 1984, for instance, the government announced that 39 new investment projects had been approved, supplying an estimated 1,600 jobs. In reality, only 14 projects were actually implemented, creating 118 jobs. The following year, the IDC approved 86 projects, expected to generate 2,220 jobs; the final total of 38 actual projects supplied 191 jobs. The gap between optimistic forecasts and poor results was a common characteristic of the NNP government's employment policy, leading to considerable scepticism when, in 1988, Blaize announced the anticipated creation of 6,000 jobs.

Unemployment is worst in the rural parishes of St David's, St Patrick's and St Mark's, where areas of extreme deprivation have been identified by aid agency workers. These areas are untouched by any expansion in manufacturing or tourism and rely almost exclusively on agriculture and fishing. While export crop prices remain buoyant and small-scale farming brings in regular cash, the situation is not yet critical for most people. Yet for many, especially young people who are not attracted to traditional agricultural work, the prospects for employment are extremely limited. According to senior trade union officials, the common safety valve for rural unemployment is emigration, and many young people have obtained 5-year visas to the US from the US embassy in Barbados, although this is becoming increasingly difficult. Figures released in September 1989 in a government paper, Grenada National Population Policy, revealed that an average of 2,000 Grenadians were emigrating annually, mostly to the US and Canada. Others move towards the capital, St George's, where prospects of work as domestic servants or factory hands are better. This has led to the growth of squatting on empty Crown Lands near St George's and additional strain on social services and amenities as embryonic shanty towns develop.

Taxing the Poor, Rewarding the Rich

The PRG's programme of social reform was linked to a policy of progressive redistributive taxation. Low earners paid no income tax at all, while medium and high earners paid 40 per cent or more after allowances. This tax scale was accompanied by the traditional duties on exports such as cocoa, nutmeg and bananas (operated since 1909) and high import taxes, payable by the small merchant class of St George's. Businesses were also heavily taxed by a company tax charged at a rate between 40 and 55 per cent of net profits. Tied to this redistributive system was the concept of a 'social wage' (encompassing free education and health and subsidised housing) as well as a state monopoly of some essential imports (certain foodstuffs, cement, drugs etc), resulting in price controls. These controls were bitterly resented by the merchant class, which had traditionally made its profits from the mark-up of imported basic goods.

USAID policy was to revitalise what it saw as an over-taxed and beleaguered private sector by radical tax reform. First, income tax rates on higher earners were reduced along with company taxes. Then, in the 1986 'Reform Budget' income tax was scrapped altogether and replaced with the 20 per cent VAT. Subsequent modifications, prompted by government inability to meet recurrent commitments, have included a further 10 per cent surcharge on goods imported from outside the CARICOM area, further VAT charges of 10 per cent payable at the wholesale and retail stages, a 2.5 per cent increase on certain price-controlled goods with a 10 per cent or less existing VAT rating, and property tax on previously excluded houses worth EC$30,000 (US$11,000) or less. In April 1989, the VAT system was again changed, with a 10 per cent tax levied on importers and manufacturers rather than wholesalers and retailers. Previously abolished taxes have reappeared under different guises, notably the export duty on farmers' produce that simply became a 2.5 per cent levy on sales by producer cooperatives.

A noticeable shift therefore took place from the USAID-approved fiscal reform package of zero income tax and high VAT to a more sales tax-oriented system, in which the government tried to recoup lost revenue and mend political damage through a range of measures and subsequent modifications.

Relief to Grenada's private sector and wealthy minority came in the form of the abolition of income tax and the relaxation of foreign exchange controls, as prescribed by USAID. This led inevitably to the hoarding of foreign currency and deposit accounts abroad. For the small group of import-export traders who make up the bulk of the island's outdated commercial class, the weakening of the Marketing and National Import Board has meant that they could return to making profits from imports that the state had briefly taken over. In response to periodic complaints from the business sector, the government introduced relief measures such as removing VAT from inputs for the local manufacturing sector.

Inevitably, indirect taxation affects the poor much more than the rich, especially if many essential items can only be obtained from outside the CARICOM area, thereby incurring an additional 10 per cent surcharge. According to critics of the tax system, such items not only include staple food products, but also school books, agricultural equipment and building materials. They also point out that the items exempted from VAT by the government are the same as the list of price-controlled goods introduced by the PRG and does not represent a new measure and indeed was only introduced after considerable public protest. The NDC, in its critique of the 1988 budget, claimed that indirect taxation triggered a price spiral which could be met by a high wage earner free of direct tax, but that was disastrous for a low earner who was previously exempt from income tax. This analysis was borne out by figures from January 1989 which showed that it took EC$1 to buy what one year earlier had cost 87 cents, even though inflation in 1988 had been only six per cent. Other figures revealed that 79 cents out of every dollar collected in taxation came from consumption taxes.

The NDC's 1990 election manifesto promised a complete overhaul of the taxation system. It claimed that an NDC government would replace the 2.5 per cent business levy with a corporation tax, reform property taxes and repeal VAT legislation. However, it emphasised that it had no intention of reintroducing personal income tax, giving rise to fears that primitive indirect taxation would continue.

Rolling Back the State

The decline in poor Grenadians' purchasing power is paralleled by a gradual drop in other living standards, notably in health, education and housing. These areas had been at the centre of the PRG's programme and had undergone significant expansion and improvement despite tough economic constraints. With Cuban and EEC assistance, the PRG set up a programme of primary and preventive health care to complement existing medical facilities. All medical and dental care became free, as did education, while innovative programmes of adult education, literacy and teacher training were widely admired. The revolutionary government initiated low-cost housing programmes and started a housing repair scheme, offering loans and grants to the low paid as a means of improving existing housing. In transport, the National Transport Service operated a fleet of 38 publicly-owned buses, providing timetabled services to rural communities ignored by commercial minibus drivers.

One of the first effects of the invasion was to drive out Cuban personnel who were assisting in the PRG health programme. They were subsequently replaced by US Peace Corps volunteers and medical personnel from Project Hope, a USAID-funded voluntary body with a controversial track record in Vietnam and Central America. Project Hope signed a seven-year agreement with the Interim Advisory Council, offering training in community health services, systems-planning and some equipment and supplies. Among the gifts-in-kind were an ultrasonic scanning machine to the General Hospital and packages of medicines, hospital furniture and medical books. The reported sum of US$10 million spent by USAID and Project Hope since 1984 has mainly gone towards the building of a new psychiatric hospital (to replace the old building at Richmond Hill destroyed during the invasion) and administration costs related to 30 doctors and other staff.

Complaints of deteriorating health services are common (US citizens are advised informally to fly to Barbados or Trinidad in the event of serious illness). The General Hospital is reportedly under-resourced, and common drugs, while theoretically free on prescription, are often unavailable. It is even rumoured that out-of-date US drugs were 'dumped' in Grenada in 1984, while USAID-donated X-ray machines were allegedly of Korean War vintage and considered by the US manufacturer fit only for use with animals. A report in October 1988 by the regional newspaper *EC News* stated that poor working conditions, broken-down equipment and low wages were forcing Grenadian nurses to work abroad in the US. Of an approved target staff of 88 nurses at the General Hospital, the report pointed out, only 50 were employed, while 20 nursing sisters were doing the work intended for 30. With such a desperate need for qualified staff, the NNP government's hostility towards Grenadians who received medical training in Cuba, organised by the PRG, was seen as perverse.

Private practice, tolerated during the PRG years, is again encouraged, with fees of EC$10 (almost equivalent to an agricultural labourer's daily wage) for a visit and EC$25 for a fuller consultation. The 1987 Budget also introduced administrative fees for X-rays, eye-tests and dental check-ups, as recommended by USAID. According to the NDC, moreover, cuts in government expenditure adversely affected medical services, as in 1988 when a health centre improvement project valued at US$250,000 was dropped. Project Hope, despite fulsome praise from the NNP Health Minister, developed an unenviable reputation for incompetence, and public squabbles emerged between Project Hope staff and personnel at the private,

US-owned St George's University School of Medicine over the use of hospital facilities and teaching.

Medical Malfeasance

Under Maurice Bishop's rule, a comprehensive primary health care system was established in Grenada, emphasizing small local health centers providing basic health care, a program of the type endorsed by both the World Health Organization and the US Agency for International Development (AID). The United States pledged, after the invasion, that it would continue operating. AID drew up plans, and the St George's Medical School offered to help run it and absorb all administrative overheads.

These plans were thwarted when William B Walsh, president of Project Hope and a Reagan crony, convinced the administration to have AID award his organization a sole-source contract to provide health care in Grenada. Project Hope has focused all its efforts on St George's Hospital [unconnected to the St George's Medical School], to which it flies US physicians for relaxing two-week stints.

Part of the reason for the administration's decision to back Walsh and ignore the primary health system may have been antipathy towards the medical school, whose administration at first refused to back Washington's fiction that its students were in need of a 'rescue mission' in October 1983. Though medical school President Charles Modica was later persuaded by the White House to be more cooperative in exchange for promises of financial assistance, still unfulfilled, the school has been boycotted by the administration. When Vice President George Bush visited the island...he refused to visit it, although he twice passed its entrance gates, turning down invitations to unveil a monument on its grounds to GIs killed in the invasion. Doctors participating in Project Hope's two-week jaunts have been under strict instructions from Walsh to avoid the medical school and shun any of its students they encounter at the hospital.

Source: Council on Hemispheric Affairs (Washington), *News and Analysis.* 21 November 1985.

In education, the post-invasion governments have reversed many of the advances achieved during the PRG years. Post-invasion policy has been towards the 'depoliticisation' of education, and this has meant abandoning the PRG's major programmes and a reduction in state commitment to education. The Centre for Popular Education (CPE), for instance, which successfully addressed the problem of functional illiteracy was immediately disbanded and replaced with the ineffectual Continuing Education Programme (CEP) which is not primarily concerned with literacy but more with skills training. Publications such as the 'Marryshow Readers' which presented Grenadian history and culture from a national perspective have been rejected as 'subversive' and replaced with imported materials. According to staff at the Teacher Training College, over 30 known PRG supporters among the country's teachers have been sacked and replaced with inexperienced staff.

The US-approved restructuring of education has involved funding some skills training and teacher training via USAID and AIFLD. It has also involved Peace Corps and other US volunteers to replace the Cuban and other personnel employed during the revolutionary period. Some scholarships to US universities are sponsored by USAID (others are available from CIDA and the European Development Fund), but critics claim that these scholarships can be vetoed by the government and often depend on political favouritism rather than merit.

The Grenada Union of Teachers complains that its members are the lowest paid (with those in Dominica) in the Eastern Caribbean. It also believes that the principle of free education for all is being seriously eroded by government policies and spending cuts. Free school books and uniforms are no longer available to children from low-income families, and school meals, which during the PRG were largely underwritten by the European Community, are now severely curtailed or stopped altogether. Some schools now raise their own funds to subsidise a school cook's wages, while others have to sell snacks and drinks to the children during breaks in order to buy essential items such as chalk. The NDC adamantly attacked the NNP government for its cuts in education spending, claiming that in 1987 only US$110,000 was allocated for supplies for 20,000 primary school children. The per capita sum of US$5.50, stated the NDC, 'is not enough to buy toilet paper for one child for one year'.

Educational standards have fallen since the invasion, and this has been reflected in examination results. In 1985, 59 per cent of Grenadian children taking Caribbean Examination Council (CXC) examinations failed; in 1986, failures rose to 61 per cent, and in 1987 to 65 per cent. 'A'-level passes at the newly founded National College (formerly the Institute of Further Education) also plummeted; in 1988 the pass rate was recorded at 40.9 per cent, but in 1989 the figure had fallen to 33.6 per cent. Declining academic results caused the Ministry of Education to form a committee to determine the causes of the problem; it reported that inadequate and poorly trained teachers, outmoded syllabi and lack of continuous assessment were all major factors. The evident lack of morale among Grenada's teachers stands in open contrast to the PRG period, when the innovative National In-Service Teacher Education Programme (NISTEP) was greeted by regional educationalists as a cost-effective and practical way of improving teachers' skills and improving standards.

As public-sector education deteriorates, private schools are growing, particularly at the primary level. With termly fees of up to US$220, these establishments are clearly beyond the reach of most Grenadians. Private schools such as Westmoreland and the Sunnyside School produce disproportionately high success rates at the Common Entrance Examination which determines competitive access to secondary school. Moreover, an article in late 1988 in the right-wing *Grenadian Voice* newspaper, advocating the return of fees for secondary education, reinforced suspicions that this was long-term government policy. The Education Minister, George McGuire, did not discount such a move. The newly established tertiary National College operates a fee-paying system.

Housing has also undergone a crisis, especially in terms of government spending. The PRG had devoted US$0.35 million a year to offering US$350 loans on easy terms to low-income families wanting to repair or improve their homes. Venezuelan cooperation had produced the first low-cost housing schemes, while the Sandino plant was intended to turn out 400 new prefabricated houses each year. The Sandino plant's private-sector replacement, Rigid Panel, collapsed without producing many houses and owing US$1 million to the state-owned Grenada Bank of Commerce. At the same time, funds for the government housing repair scheme were cut dramatically from US$0.55 million in 1987 to US$185,000 in 1988, even though beneficiaries from the PRG period were asked to continue repayment of their loans. In 1987 although US$1 million was budgeted to be spent on new low-cost housing, the opposition NDC claimed that not one house was actually built. A government-commissioned report of 1986 reveals the extent of the housing problem in Grenada.

Housing

According to a government report, carried out by an expert from the Commonwealth Fund for Technical Cooperation, Grenada's housing requires huge investment in order to raise standards from near slum conditions. The report contains the following statistics:

■ Of a total of 21,016 registered homes, 32 per cent are comprised of one or two rooms.

■ 40 per cent of houses contain between 5 and 13 people.

■ 33 per cent are considered totally unfit for human habitation.

■ 61 per cent are made of wood.

■ 34 per cent depend on water from public standpipes, while 17 per cent depend on rain collection and wells.

■ 62 per cent have pit latrines.

Noting that Grenada's housing requirement up to the end of the 1990s will be approximately 14,000 new units, the report recommended that the government strengthen the PRG-designed House Repair Programme 'to provide more funds to households to carry out more sytematic repairs and to provide for toilet and bath.' Government spending on the House Repair Programme has in fact dropped since the publication of the report.

Source: National Democratic Congress, *Cry Deliverance!* April 1988.

What's in a Name?

The NNP government and the interim regime before it did their utmost to remove visible reminders of the PRG's popular social programmes. At a crude level, they simply renamed services and institutions, while continuing to maintain them, albeit at reduced levels. Thus, the National Transport Service (NTS) was rebaptised the Public Transport Service (PTS). Similarly, the Centre for Popular Education (CPE) became the Continuing Education Programme (CEP), while the National In-Service Teacher Education Programme (NISTEP) was renamed the In-Service Teacher Education Programme (INSTEP). Changes in acronyms have been accompanied by budget cuts. The PTS is popularly seen as run down and unreliable, and has only been saved by the arrival of new buses from Venezuela. CEP and INSTEP, meanwhile, have been significantly downgraded from the importance allotted to CPE and NISTEP by the revolutionary government.

Yet the post-invasion administrations, while criticising the PRG for alleged financial mismanagement, have been all too willing to accept credit for programmes and initiatives undertaken during the revolution. Several years after its overthrow, some of the revolution's major achievements are only now coming on stream, while foreign assistance negotiated by the PRG is still arriving. The international airport, for instance, was incontestably the creation of the PRG and has been instrumental in the growth of tourism. Yet neither the interim government nor the NNP ever officially recognised this fact and both rejected persistent calls for Point Salines airport to be renamed after Maurice Bishop. The four rural medical stations were built with Swedish aid sought by the PRG in 1983, but came into use during the NNP administration. Equally, projects for rural feeder roads, the western main road and low-cost housing predated the NNP regime but were finished during its period in office.

The incorporation of PRG policies into the NNP government's list of 'achievements' did not escape the notice of the *Financial Times* in its special report of December 1986:

> For all that they rail against the Bishop administration, many of the NNP's agricultural policies are extensions of those contracted by their predecessor who, despite the Marxist rhetoric, had obtained a high degree of confidence among the western donors who backed their schemes.

By taking on some of the principal commitments and plans of the PRG, the NNP government, particularly before the split of December 1986, inherited the vestiges of a coherent development strategy that it would not have set in motion of its own accord. With additional large amounts of US aid, it was initially able to sustain elements of this strategy, while its US paymasters forced it to abandon those welfare programmes that it considered 'statist'. Gradually, however, as US assistance has fallen, so too has government expenditure on social services and capital investment.

Grenada's hidden destitution

At 23, Rholda George already has five children, but she has never worked. She left school at 13 when she gave birth to her first child and lacks the skills that would make her employable in Grenada's competitive job market. Her mother, who used to take care of the children from the pittance she earned, has also joined the unemployment statistics following a recent surgical operation.

Four of the five children are attending school, albeit with limited supplies of text and exercise books and without shoes on their feet. The uniforms they wear are the donations of generous neighbours. The last child, now more than a year old, is still unable to walk, probably lacking the nourishment and energy to attempt to do so. It sits in the yard, engaged in an involuntary game with swarms of flies...

It is particularly easy to miss such destitution when one visits Telescope, a village on the outskirts of Grenada's east coast town of Grenville. For Telescope is a burgeoning residential district with modern houses 'worth a fortune' going up all around... But in one of the side streets is an extended family familiar with the scourge of poverty and the pangs of hunger. 'It might sound strange' [says St Andrews Lions Club member Yolande Joseph], 'but there are a lot of people around our country who do not know where the next meal's coming from. If you go to Seamoon and the back of La Poterie you will find a lot of those', she reported.

Source: EC News, 3 November 1989

This has meant the steady erosion of the gains made during the PRG years. In early 1989, for instance, the government introduced legislation to amend a PRG law of 1980 which introduced statutory maternity leave for the first time in Grenada. Under the PRG legislation, any woman with 18 months service was entitled to two months maternity leave on full pay and another month without. The NNP legislation, prompted by the Grenada Chamber of Commerce,

Day care nursery built by PRG, 1982

reduced the employers' legal commitment to only 40 per cent of full pay for the two months. Equally revealing was a UN Economic and Social Council report, published in May 1989, which pointed out that Grenada's population had an average intake of calories, protein and vitamin A below recommended levels for the period 1983-5. In particular, the report claimed, Grenadians' intake of vitamin A was less than half that of Barbadians and lower even than that of Haitians, thereby creating a real risk of malnutrition. No explicit connection between these statistics, the post-invasion increase in food prices and the abandonment of free milk schemes was made by the report, but it would be difficult to see this as merely coincidental.

Examples such as these are representative of the shift in priorities that has reversed the progress made by poor Grenadians during the revolution. Vestiges of the welfare programmes remain, and some USAID-funded schemes such as the 'Special Development Activities' programme are derived from PRG policies, but many of the revolution's reforms have disappeared altogether. The result has been the return of institutionalised social inequality.

Handed over to the vagaries of market forces, Grenada's fragile economy has been subjected to extensive privatisation and deregulation. It has survived, partly due to favourable world prices for its exports and partly because of extensive foreign aid. But neither of these factors can be relied upon over the long term. According to the logic of the market, Grenada must learn to be financially viable and self-sustaining. With the twin spectres of reduced US aid and the loss of preferential markets in the new Europe, such objectives appear increasingly impossible.

In the meantime, an unfair and ineffective tax system, imposed on the poor to benefit the private sector, has caused genuine hardship and forced the NNP government several times to the edge of literal bankruptcy. US pressure to further cut the public sector could lead either to increased unemployment and political tension, or to a refusal on the government's part and resulting economic sanctions from the US. Budget deficits, caused in part by the imposition of unworkable taxation schemes, lead inevitably to cuts in government spending and more redundancies. The end result for any US-sponsored government is a dilemma: either to push through more USAID-approved 'reforms', hence further alienating public opinion, or to risk US displeasure by reducing the speed of restructuring. As US largesse dries up, the latter course may be the lesser of two evils.

For Richer, for Poorer: Comparison of Pre and Post Invasion Governments

Issue	PRG	US/post-invasion
Type of Society	Mixed	Dependent Capitalist
Dominant Sector	State	Private (especially foreign capital) privatised state assets
Participation	Direct involvement through trade unions, mass organisations and local councils. Criticised for elitist party structure and not holding elections	Elections once every 5 years
Housing	Low-cost housing for the poor. Government loans to poor families for house improvements	Cuts in government repair scheme. Few new low-cost homes built.
Health care	Free medical and dental treatment. New medical centres built. 14% of government budget (1982-3)	Conditions deteriorating. Charges for check-ups, X rays introduced. Private practice now encouraged
Education	Brought in free primary and secondary schooling. Free uniforms and books to children of poor families. 22% of government budget (1982-3)	Adult literacy programmes cut back. Scholarships to US replace those to Cuba. Cuts to free uniforms books and meals. Exam results get worse. Rise in private schools

Jobs	State-sector jobs cut unemployment from estimated 49% to 14%	Huge job losses as state is cut back. Private investment fails to compensate. Unemployment up to 30% by mid 1984
Women's rights	Set up Ministry of Women's Affairs. Brought in paid maternity leave, children's pre-school and day centres	Statutory maternity pay cut back
Foreign policy	Non-aligned. Pro-Cuba	US-dominated
Prices	Basic imported and domestically produced goods controlled	Most controls removed, leading to food price increases
Taxation	Mainly income tax. Poorer earners pay no tax. Heavy tax on company profits. Duties on major exports	Reduce income tax, especially on high earners. Bring in sales taxes, damaging living standards of the poor
Agriculture	Built up state and cooperative sectors; diversified range of crops and undertook limited processing of conserves	Shift to private sector, selling off state farms. Failed attempt to increase the number of private smallholders

Chapter 4
In the Name of Freedom

'Those who use [the term invasion] are putting our society in jeopardy. It was not an oppressive incursion upon an unwilling population. We went in to free people; the Soviets went into Afghanistan to enslave people.'
Charles Z. Wick, head of US Information Agency, November 1983.

'If you don't watch out, we might take from you the privilege of standing there and making that noise.'
Foreign Minister Ben Jones addressing hecklers at public meeting, August 1986.

The rhetoric surrounding the US invasion was one of liberation. Eagerly picking up the phrase coined by Grenadian journalist Alister Hughes, President Reagan referred to the military action as a 'rescue mission'. (Initially he described it as an invasion; subsequently, it has been euphemistically redefined as an 'intervention', thereby removing connotations of militarism, resistance and the violation of national sovereignty). Who was rescued from what, however, was open to different interpretations. For Hughes, the rescue entailed literal release from imprisonment by the shortlived RMC, which had arrested him and other alleged 'counter-revolutionaries'. For Reagan, the term fitted with the stage-managed return of the US medical students from Grenada (the great majority of whom had felt themselves to be in no danger until the invasion itself). More generally, the image of salvation was one that the Reagan administration wished to apply to the end of the revolution and Grenada's return to the US fold. Within the administration's ideological frame of reference, Grenada had been 'freed' from communism.

Much of the related US propaganda attack on the revolution, both before and after the invasion, focused specifically on the PRG's human rights record. In particular, the US accused the Bishop regime of a range of violations, including arbitrary arrest, imprisonment and torture. Washington also berated the PRG for censorship, repression of religious freedoms, general harassment of political opponents and failure to hold democratic elections.

Given these allegations, the human rights and democratic record of the US-backed interim regime and NNP government deserves particular scrutiny, since both appointed and elected administrations claimed credit for a return to basic freedoms. However, critics of Grenada's post-invasion governments point out that a range of civil and political rights — trade unionism, democratic self-expression, legal, constitutional and employment rights — have in fact been eroded since October 1983 rather than the reverse.

Human Rights

For many supporters of the revolution, the PRG's response to internal opposition was its least palatable characteristic. It is well documented that during the four-and-a-half year period of the revolution, some 3,000 people were held for questioning, of whom about one-tenth were detained, usually for two or three days. On 26 October 1983, there were over 100 political prisoners at Richmond Hill prison, although many of these had been detained under the draconian curfew imposed by the RMC junta. According to Amnesty International's annual reports for the period 1979-83, a figure of between 75 and 100 political prisoners remained more or less constant, of whom six had been held since the NJM's insurrection in March 1979. Amnesty also expressed concern over alleged ill-treatment of prisoners and the death sentence passed on four people convicted of bombing offences in November 1982.

The PRG and its supporters argued that stringent security was necessary in the face of a CIA-inspired destabilisation plan, similar to that experienced in Allende's Chile and Manley's Jamaica. In particular, they claimed that known conservatives and pro-US agents were conspiring to attack the revolution through disinformation, economic sabotage and terrorist activity. The bomb which exploded on 19 June 1980 at a government rally, killing three young women and injuring 100 more bystanders, seemed to support this view. It led to the arrest of two members of the Budhlall family and the alleged discovery of links between these former NJM activists and CIA operatives inside and outside Grenada. Other legitimate security concerns were members of Gairy's thuggish 'Mongoose Gang', who had acted as armed equivalents to the Duvaliers' notorious Tontons Macoutes in Haiti.

Yet others admitted that the PRG over-reacted, confusing legitimate political opponents with spies and security threats. Occasionally, outspoken but law-abiding critics of the revolution were harassed, suffering house arrest and restriction of movement. The local churches, for instance, while for the most part conservative and suspicious of the PRG's support for the regional exponents of liberation theology, hardly merited close government scrutiny. At the same time, petty criminals were routinely detained, especially before major rallies and conferences, when foreign dignitaries were expected. Rastafarians were also seen as a security risk and were subjected to particularly harsh treatment from the PRG's security forces. Rising to a full-time strength of 600, sections of the PRA had a reputation for arrogance and for an over-zealous approach towards 'revolutionary manners' (discipline).

The week of RMC rule, preceded by the Fort Rupert massacre, marked the lowest point in democratic rights before the invasion. The

Philip Wolmuth

US troops guard a political prisoner, March 1984

almost permanent curfew, the news blackout and the sweeping arrests of Bishop supporters and other apparent dissidents numbering over 500 created a climate of terror that reinforced the sense of trauma surrounding the deaths of Bishop and the others. In reality, no proven human rights violations other than detention took place after the massacre, yet such was the state of fear that many Grenadians welcomed the US invasion.

The euphoria caused by the fall of the RMC could not, however, conceal the fact that the invasion and ensuing occupation entailed gross violations not only of national sovereignty, but also of basic rights. As the fighting subsided, the occupying US and Caribbean Peacekeeping Force personnel engaged in sweeping arrests of those suspected of NJM or PRA membership. The Cuban construction workers who had resisted an attack on their quarters at the international airport were subjected to particularly humiliating treatment. Some 600 of them were held for days in barbed wire enclosures exposed to the elements, where they were interrogated by US intelligence officers. Similar treatment was handed out to hundreds of Grenadians, but in many cases their conditions of imprisonment were even worse. Such treatment was in direct contravention of the Geneva Convention and, according to Amnesty International, violated internationally accepted standards.

The Rescue Mission

NJM members in public service had been particularly badly treated. One such person told us about being picked up twice by the US forces, and how he had been tortured on the second occasion by Dominican soldiers under American supervision. He had been throttled twice and threatened with drowning, the marks were still visible on his neck. While detained at Point Salines, he had seen people being kept in wooden crates. Many prisoners had been beaten and people were forced to lie in muddy ditches and crawl on their bellies. By the serial number on his card it was clear that around 2,000 people had been held at the Salines Detention Camp. All were issued with a green card on release (by the printing and spelling on it, probably printed outside the country by US officials) under the heading of the 'combined military forces detainees compound liason (sic) officer'. This card informs the reader that the holder is not to be picked up within the next 15 days, unless he or she engages in 'anti-government activity'. Some people at the camp were asked if they would 'work for the CIA', and the main purpose of interrogation was information on people in the NJM, and how it was organised. The whole security operation was in this way being aimed

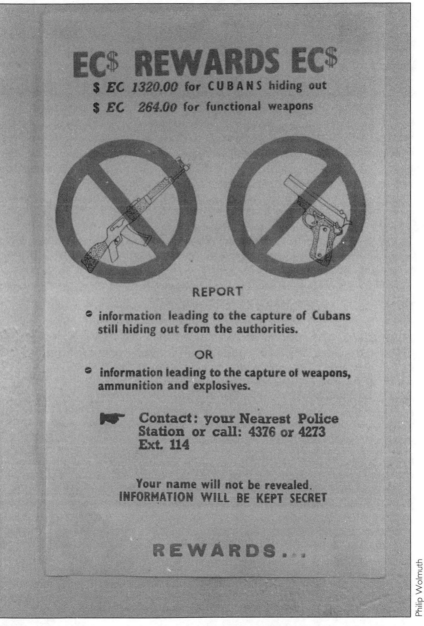

Wall poster, 1984

against the NJM, and not at the apprehension of those responsible for the killings on October 19th.

Source: Grenada: Report of a British Labour Movement Delegation, December 1983, p.22.

Some 1,000 Grenadians were rounded up in the first weeks of the occupation, and the information received was recorded in US data bases. At a press conference, Major-General Jack Farris explained the rationale behind the 'anti-subversion' programme:

> You develop a human intelligence network, whereby you have your police and your agents throughout the country and find out who the bad guys are... You build a data base on those people, on thousands of them, and bring them all in and pick up all these people and question them. You put them all in a data base, and that's how you stamp out something like that.

People selected for interrogation included not only PRA members and known supporters of the RMC, but also key figures in the former PRG regime and NJM supporters. At roadblocks and the airport, US and CPF troops carried lists of alleged sympathisers, and according to the London-based *Guardian,* former members of the Mongoose Gang, eager for revenge, joined the occupying forces in house-to-house searches. Allegations of ill treatment at the hand of these troops were commonplace. Notices appeared offering US$100 for PRA guns and US$500 for details of Cuban personnel in Grenada. A Preventive Detention Ordinance came into effect on 15 November, allowing the recently constituted Advisory Council to detain any person without charge, subject to the non-binding advice of an independent tribunal.

Among those arrested were a number of NJM Central Committee members and PRA personnel, associated with the crisis within the party and the ensuing violence and military coup. Bernard and Phyllis Coard were taken aboard US warships, where, they claimed, they were beaten and interrogated. In total, all 15 members of the RMC were held, together with the Coards and several other key political figures. It was not until February 1984, however, that the government brought murder charges against 19 individuals, after dropping an earlier attempt to charge them under PRG anti-terrorism legislation. The precise status of the accused and the legal grounds for their detention by foreign military forces was controversial and was to remain so throughout the long trial and appeal procedures.

Ironically, as NJM members and sympathisers were rounded up and interrogated, the government pardoned and released many of those imprisoned by the PRG. These included not only members of Gairy's Mongoose Gang, but also Kenneth and Kennedy Budhlall, imprisoned for their part in the 1980 Queen's Park bombing. After a pardon from Governor-General Scoon, the Budhlall brothers swiftly dropped their self-proclaimed anarchism to take prominent positions in the NNP. The charge of CIA involvement in their activity was never refuted, and their subsequent role in alleged improprieties surrounding a USAID-financed road-building project has yet to be clarified.

Psychological Warfare

Despite considerable incompetence, the US military victory of October 1983 was never in doubt. There remained a psychological and ideological war to be fought, however, for the 'hearts and minds' of the majority of Grenadians. With the invasion force came Psychological

Philip Wolmuth

Graffiti in St George's, allegedly the work of PSYOPS

Operations staff (PSYOPS) from Fort Bragg, determined to eradicate support for the revolution. Working with the CIA, the PSYOPS teams faced a difficult task in that they were expected to discredit the revolution and its leaders, while recognising popular respect and affection for Maurice Bishop. The arrests made, however, were indiscriminate, including prominent Bishop supporters such as Kendrick Radix and George Louison who had themselves been detained by the RMC.

PSYOPS took over Radio Free Grenada's frequency (the station itself had been bombed) and set up Spice Island Radio, transmitting a mix of US rock music and propaganda. Posters and bulletin boards were placed around the island, showing Bernard Coard and General Hudson Austin, the Chairman of the RMC, blindfolded and semi-naked, under the statement 'these criminals attempted to sell Grenada out to the communists'. The media attack on the revolution was soon joined by the right-wing *Grenadian Voice* newspaper, which the PRG had closed after one issue in June 1981 on grounds of anti-state activity. Supported by several regional conservative newspapers, the *Grenadian Voice* began a series of articles, naming Bishop sympathisers and condemning 'communism'. Some of the allegations levelled against the PRG, however, notably those of corruption and financial mismanagement, proved to be highly unpopular and were rapidly abandoned. Other rumours were altogether more imaginative; the discovery of a stock of overalls at a government agricultural training centre led to the 'revelation' that the PRG was planning to enslave Grenadians and introduce forced collectivisation in the same way as Pol Pot's regime in Kampuchea.

The occupying forces seized bundles of documents from government offices and sent them back to the US. Parts of this haul were subsequently published or passed on to approved US academics and journalists for inclusion in their analyses of the revolution. Typical of these publications was *Grenada: The Untold Story*, co-authored by a State Department officer, which promised to demonstrate that 'Grenada was well on its way to becoming a Soviet puppet state in a strategically vital region of the eastern Caribbean.' Generally, the documents were used selectively — and unconvincingly — to justify the US invasion. Although some of the documents were returned in May 1985, the legal grounds for the wholesale confiscation of a sovereign nation's government papers remain, to say the least, controversial.

Grenada: The Untold Story peddled the officially condoned US line on Maurice Bishop, portraying the revolution's leader as a committed Marxist who successfully hid his political agenda behind a veneer of social-democratic moderation. According to Mark Krischik, a PSYOPS specialist seconded from the US embassy in Buenos Aires, who spoke to journalists in December 1983, 'Bishop was as much of a God-damned communist as those God-damned communists in Richmond Hill prison, and our job is to make the Grenadians understand this.' This version of events, however, soon gave way to another which painted Bishop as a well-meaning if inept idealist who was overthrown by a vicious group of extremists. This view became more prominent and widespread during the murder trial, when local media and US sources attacked Coard *et al* as 'Marxists' as opposed to Bishop who was merely a 'leftist'. This distinction had already been much used at the time of the invasion itself in order to depict the situation in Grenada as one of dangerous political polarisation.

PSYOPS Problem: the Bishop Factor

The trickiest problem that the US 'hearts and minds' battle faced (and still faces) was the one on account of Grenadian memory. Maurice Bishop, the principal target of the US pre-invasion PSYOPS effort, had as a result of the invasion and the events of mid-October 1983, become a hero and a martyr. His memory became an ideological stumbling block in US attempts to consolidate their position. The attempts of the post-invasion regime to block his popular socio-economic measures such as free school education and free milk for school children endeared him further. The US PSYOPS people were, however, quick to recognize the danger, and they wisely altered their stance. A 'revisionist view' of the 'Castroite Bishop' was widely voiced. Colonel Jim Ashworth, the head of the Psychological Operation in Grenada, went to the extent of describing Maurice Bishop, the ex-PM, as 'a very charismatic figure' whose 'death was very tragic'. By December 1983, polls showed that over 50 per cent of Grenada's youth thought 'on balance' that the PRG was good for Grenada. By March 1984, Bishop's supporters were emboldened enough to launch a party named after him.

Source: Vijay Tiwathia, *The Grenada War: Anatomy of a Low-Intensity Conflict*, pp.145-6.

Crude anti-communist agitation was particularly in evidence at the time of the December 1984 election. A lurid and fantastically inaccurate pamphlet, entitled *Grenada: Rescued from Rape and Slavery* and printed

Extract from *Rescued From Rape and Slavery*

in New York by an extreme right-wing group, was widely circulated. This wave of anti-communist propaganda coincided with the NNP's election campaign which caricatured the MBPM as dangerous extremists.

With the advent of the trial, the verdict and the subsequent appeal, anti-communist propaganda has been mainly aimed at Coard and the other defendants. Bishop himself has been partly rehabilitated, even by the NNP government, which in October 1988 held a brief and vague commemorative ceremony at the scene of his execution. To this extent, Bishop's memory is used against those convicted of his murder. The NNP government and media also regularly attacked the MBPM, which claims to uphold Bishop's legacy, seeking to link the party to the idea of international terrorism and communist 'conspiracy'. A government press release, dutifully reprinted in Grenada's various newspapers in July 1988, claimed that the MBPM had recently 'sent representatives to Panama where talks were held with agents of Colonel Gadafi [sic] and agents acting as bodyguard and advisor to General Manuel Norriega [sic].'

The Trial
The trial, conviction and appeal of former NJM, RMC and PRA members have been much more dominated by constitutional and legal details than by any clear revelation of the circumstances surrounding the death of Maurice Bishop and ten others. Of the original 20 defendants, one was released at the Preliminary Inquiry and one was pardoned provided he turned witness for the prosecution. The remaining 18 defendants were eventually brought to trial in April 1986 after a long series of legal wrangles and postponements, and on 4 December, 14 were found guilty of murder, three of manslaughter, while one was acquitted on all charges. The 14 were sentenced to hang; the three were given extraordinarily long sentences of 30 to 45 years imprisonment.

The defendants insisted throughout the proceedings that the Grenada Supreme Court which was trying them was unconstitutional. The Appeals Court ruled that although indeed unconstitutional, the Supreme Court was temporarily legal under the 'doctrine of state necessity'. Ironically, the defendants' case rested on the fact that the PRG itself had established the Supreme Court, having withdrawn Grenada from the Eastern Caribbean judicial system. This meant that Grenadians no longer had the right of final appeal to the Judicial Committee of the Privy Council in the United Kingdom (People's Law

No.84 of 1979, Privy Council [Abolition of Appeals] Law, 1979). Now, however, the defendants claimed that right for themselves, since the post-invasion reinstatement of the 1974 constitution implied the return to the pre-PRG legal system. That the defendants were arguing to be tried by a system that they themselves had abolished when in power was seen by many Grenadians as lacking consistency.

Refusing to recognise the jurisdiction of the Court, the defendants declined to take part in the trial, offering no formal defence. The defence team of 12 barristers withdrew just before the trial began, in protest at alleged irregularities, and the defendants made no sworn statements and cross-examined no witnesses. Instead, the case of the accused rested on the allegedly unconstitutional nature of the Court and on a further series of apparent irregularities. These included:

— the 'arbitrary' selection of Judge Denis Byron on secondment from the judiciary of the OECS to hear this specific case on a short-term contract;
— the dismissal of the Court Registrar and his replacement by Denise Campbell, who until that point had been a member of the prosecution team;
— an improper selection of jurors, some of whom had allegedly jeered and booed the defendants;
— the removal from the defendants' prison cells of papers relevant to the trial. Some of these papers were allegedly later returned, having been copied;
— the removal from Grenada of the government documents, which, the defendants claimed, would help to substantiate their innocence.

The defendants made other allegations during the course of the trial involving ill-treatment (regular beatings, poor diet, solitary confinement, withholding of visits and letters and insufficient access to legal counsel) in the Richmond Hill prison. Lionel Maloney, the Barbados-born and US-appointed Commissioner of Prisons, denied all such allegations, but Amnesty International repeatedly expressed its concern over reports of ill-treatment. The defendants' insistence that certain statements used in evidence against them had been obtained by torture has not yet been independently confirmed.

While several independent sources concur that many such irregularities took place in the trial, other alleged violations of the defendants' rights are more open to question. Ramsey Clark, a former US Attorney-General who has campaigned on the issue, stated, for instance, that the case 'proceeded to trial without any defense counsel present' (*Liberation*, London, March/April 1987). 'The defendants', writes Clark, 'were prevented from defending themselves. They were held in a bus outside the court room throughout all the prosecution testimony.' According to Amnesty International, however, 'the defence lawyers withdrew from the case at the request of the defendants' (*Amnesty International Report* 1987), and most of the defendants 'were removed from the courtroom each day, after disrupting the proceedings by chanting.' Amnesty International continues: 'most of the witness testimony for the prosecution was therefore given in the absence of the accused. Summaries of the testimony were read to the defendants by the trial judge but they declined to cross-examine the witnesses.'

Clark also asserted that the courtroom inside the Richmond Hill prison perimeter constitutes 'an inherently prejudicial location'. However, when the defendants appeared in the St George's Crown Court in 1984, a violent demonstration was directed against them, resulting in injury to a police officer. This usual court, moreover, can only accommodate a maximum of six or seven defendants, according to the authorities.

Supporters of the defendants have frequently accused the Grenadian government of presiding over a 'show trial', of arranging, in Ramsey Clark's words, 'a protracted, manipulated, one-sided effort to further falsify history.' In particular, they claim that the authorities allowed, and even encouraged, massive pre-trial propaganda against the accused. They also accuse the US of underwriting the cost of the legal process by offering the Grenadian government US$5.5 million as a special grant at the time of President Reagan's visit to the island in February 1986. (There is some ambiguity here, since President Reagan's grant was specifically made to the Eastern Caribbean judicial system, to which Grenada does not currently belong). Others, meanwhile, have pointed out that the defendants have received free legal aid for the lawyers of their choice, costing the Grenadian government more than US$1 million out of a total estimated trial and appeal bill exceeding US$4 million.

For a supposed 'show trial', the legal proceedings have been extremely drawn out, messy and inconclusive. The evidence against the accused was largely circumstantial and often questionable, the defence case contradictory and almost non-existent. As the trial dragged on, so public apathy in Grenada grew. Initial desires for judicial vengeance gave way to more widespread indifference. The sentences themselves, according to observers, provoked little reaction in Grenada, even though Prime Minister Blaize called for troop reinforcements from the SSU forces of other OECS countries to be present in Grenada at the trial's close. If it was ever intended as a clean and efficient operation in what the Defence Lawyer Ian Ramsay has called 'judicial murder', the trial has clearly failed.

Instead, the Bishop murder trial became an embarrassment to the Grenadian government and to the region as a whole. When in March 1988, Grenada applied to rejoin the Eastern Caribbean court system, Prime Minister Blaize was informed by OECS Chairman John Compton that the timing of the request was inappropriate. This was widely interpreted as a desire on the part of the OECS to disassociate itself from the trial and the ensuing appeal. The appeal, which started in May 1988, was still at the beginning of 1990 repeating the constitutional arguments that dominated the trial itself. But it also began to contest the prosecution evidence the defendants had initially ignored. With the sudden death of Court of Appeal president, J.O.F. Haynes, in December 1988 the appeal seemed set to stretch further into the future, especially since the defendants had instructed their lawyers to concentrate on evidence as well as constitutional points. In the meantime, Phyllis Coard complained in a book written in prison of systematic ill-treatment, and several defendants went on hunger strikes to publicise their case.

Legal Rights

The Bishop murder trial has not been the only controversial legal event to take place in post-invasion Grenada. When the US tried to extradite Chester Humphrey, a well-known NJM activist and TAWU vice-president, it exposed several unsavoury aspects of the legal system. Humphrey had been charged in 1979 in the US with arms smuggling (allegedly importing weapons into Grenada which were used in the anti-Gairy insurrection), but had jumped bail and returned to Grenada. With the invasion, Humphrey, like other NJM activists, was immediately arrested. Released without charge after six-and-a-half months, he was re-arrested two months later, subject to an extradition request from the US government.

The US authorities claimed that an extradition agreement between Grenada and the US existed, based on a British colonial arrangement and an untraceable memorandum from Prime Minister Gairy to the UN. Previously, this treaty had only led to an impasse when the PRG had tried to use it to extradite Gairy from exile in the US to face charges of corruption. This time, the US won its request in a first hearing, which the Supreme Court then upheld. In January 1986, however, the Court of Appeal overturned the extradition order after it was heard that insufficient evidence, a clause on political offences and a five-year statute of limitations all made the extradition proceedings invalid.

Humphrey's release was presented by the NNP government as evidence of an independent Grenadian judiciary. However, an international campaign and a 59-day hunger strike by Humphrey had focused attention on the case and its blatant irregularities and probably had more to do with his release. The revelation that the US government had made payments of US$4,000 to two senior Grenadian civil servants for their assistance in the extradition case undermined international confidence in the legal proceedings, while Humphrey's widely circulated letters from prison painted a scandalous picture of deprivation. Altogether, the unsuccessful attempt to invoke a non-existent extradition treaty and the prolonged detention without charge of a Grenadian citizen raised serious questions about the island's legal system.

A Climate of Violence

'[Grenada's] 800-man US-trained police force has acquired a reputation for brutality, arbitrary arrests, and abuse of authority.' So concluded the Washington-based Council on Hemispheric Affairs in a November 1985 analysis of human rights in Grenada. According to the MBPM, six Grenadians died in incidents involving the security forces between April 1984 and January 1986 and two since, shot in the streets of St George's; no inquests or inquiries were forthcoming. Among these documented incidents was the death of Ernest John at Grenville police station, allegedly caused by a US Marine. In a settlement, John's family was reportedly paid US$370 by the US authorities. Other reports have detailed harassment and arrest of political activists, including supporters of the Chester Humphrey campaign. When President Reagan visited Grenada in February 1986, for instance, police and SSU units arrested 25 people in a raid on a poor area in St George's, apparently because an anti-Reagan poster was prominently displayed as part of a protest against the visit. The police beat their prisoners and demolished several wooden shacks.

Despite strong-arm tactics by the police and SSU, crime has risen alarmingly since the US invasion. Much of it is drug-related, involving smuggling between Grenada and other destinations, notably Trinidad. Several murders, including that of Madonna Swan in January 1987, are reputedly linked to the drug trade, and unsubstantiated rumours link such criminal activity to prominent political figures. The NNP government blamed violent crime on former PRA personnel and 'leftist elements', who are still allegedly armed. Robberies and shootings have escalated, and complaints of police incompetence are commonplace, despite the doubling of the police budget since 1983. Critics of government social policy point out that the priority has been on paramilitary 'national security' rather than criminal investigation.

The climate of violence was vividly exemplified in June 1989, when an Assistant Commissioner of Police shot dead not only his superior but also a US political officer in a dispute over the misappropriation of funds for a regional military exercise. Almost as disturbing as the incident itself was the ambiguity surrounding the death of the Assistant Commissioner, who was variously reported to have been shot, beaten to death or died of cardiac arrest.

In response to what it saw as politically motivated unrest, the NNP government enacted several draconian pieces of legislation. In June 1986, it obtained parliamentary approval for an emergency powers bill, giving the security forces sweeping powers of arrest, detention without trial and curfew. In response to opposition complaints that the legislation resembled the repressive measures introduced by Gairy in the 1970s, Attorney-General Ben Jones argued that arms and ammunition from the PRG period were still in circulation and could be used to 'subvert the country'. This legislation had already been preceded by the Restriction of Movement Act, aimed at preventing travel into and from Grenada by those 'whose aims, tendencies or objectives include the overthrow of the democratic and Parliamentary system of Government'. Even before this legislation was passed, immigration officials seized the passport of MBPM deputy leader, Einstein Louison, as he attempted to leave the island for meetings abroad in May 1985. His passport was finally returned in December 1988.

Apart from seeking to obstruct a legal political party's international business, the NNP government also passed legislation against the trade union movement which it saw as a potential source of political opposition. Alongside the harassment of Chester Humphrey and the unsuccessful AIFLD campaign, anti-union activity took the form of the proposed re-enactment of the Essential Services Act, first introduced in 1964, amended and extended by Gairy in 1978 and repealed by the PRG in 1979. Under the terms of this law, workers in areas deemed by government to be essential are forbidden to strike, while others are obliged to give 28 days notice of any industrial action. Recognition of unions was also denied, and the TUC accused the government of trying to subvert free collective bargaining procedures and interfering in individual unions' internal business. When members of the TAWU, GUT and PWU demonstrated in June 1989, protesting against the government's refusal to discuss the three-year-old pay dispute, armed SSU personnel and police blocked off streets leading to the centre of St George's, while helicopter gunships flew overhead.

'National Security'

Perceiving itself as threatened by political subversion, the NNP government, like the interim administration before it, often resorted to restricting the rights of its presumed opponents. Expulsions, bannings, confiscation of literature and censorship all featured in its 'national security' repertoire. Particular targets have been individuals connected with the NJM or MBPM, but foreign journalists and regional organisations with no specific political allegiance have also been affected.

After the initial post-invasion purge of foreign workers and advisors by the US occupation force, official suspicion has been directed at journalists researching 'sensitive' subjects. In April 1984, for example, a US radio reporter, Don Foster, was expelled after investigating the death in police custody of Rodney Charles. After Foster's expulsion, it emerged that a former Radio Free Grenada correspondent had been refused entry from St Lucia. In December that year, two Canadians involved in establishing community agricultural projects were deported. As the MBPM has attempted to hold conferences and international meetings, invited guests and speakers have been refused entry to Grenada or otherwise harassed. In May 1988, the MBPM's first convention was marred by the expulsion of Trinidad Oil Workers' Union executive member David Abdulah and former press secretary to Maurice Bishop, Don Rojas. Another invited participant, Temba Ntinga of the African National Congress, was held at the international airport for several hours before being admitted. In October 1989 Trinidad-born Kwame Toure (formerly Stokely Carmichael) was deported from the island, where he was attending a MBPM rally.

In the aftermath of the 1988 controversy, unnamed official sources admitted that an extensive government list of 'undesirables' existed. Allegedly containing the names of several well-known Caribbean political activists — Tim Hector of Antigua, Trevor Munroe of Jamaica, Rosie Douglas of Dominica and George Odlum of St Lucia — the list also included, sources stated, former Attorney-General Richard Hart and respected regional journalist Rickey Singh. Subsequent government denials specifically mentioned Singh, a prominent critic of the US invasion whose Barbadian work permit was temporarily withdrawn by the Adams government for his opposition to the US action.

'Subversive' publications have also been intercepted by immigration officials, most notably a consignment of books sent to the MBPM by Pathfinder Press, a left-wing publisher. Among the seized titles were an anthology of speeches by Maurice Bishop, books by or about Nelson Mandela, Fidel Castro and Malcolm X, and an anthology of political writing edited by Don Rojas. In its defence, the government invoked a decree dating from 1951 and the colonial period, controlling the distribution of political literature. In a similar vein, the interim government had tried to obstruct the printing of the MBPM's weekly newspaper, the *Indies Times*, under the terms of the Newspaper Amendment Act of 1978, a law passed by the Gairy regime to prevent opposition newspapers from operating. Another case of censorship has involved the seizure of Phyllis Coard's diary of prison life, published in London and confiscated by immigration officials on arrival in Grenada. The NNP government banned not only Marx and Lenin, but, surprisingly, Graham Greene's comic novel, *Our Man in Havana*.

Government sensitivity towards what it takes as criticism was occasionally taken to absurd lengths. In July 1987, *Newsweek* reported that a commission had been set up to vet the traditionally political calypsos that were played on the radio. The Ministry of Culture had reportedly issued a directive that the state radio should not broadcast calypsos containing 'politically sensitive matters that cannot be substantiated'. The directive followed an incident in which a radio announcer was suspended for playing the well-known calypso, 'The Sinking Ship', shortly after a news bulletin announcing the resignation of three government ministers. In July 1985 the SSU also forcibly closed a 'pirate' radio station, despite the owners' possession of a government licence. More generally, opposition parties such as the NDC and the MBPM complained that they were denied access to the state-owned media.

The NNP government was equally touchy in its response to a reported 'poverty survey' being carried out in Grenada in 1988 by the Caribbean Conference of Churches (CCC). Claiming that non-governmental organisations were seeking to destabilise Grenada, the government accused the CCC of singling out Grenada for criticism on such matters as unemployment. The controversy was dampened, however, when the CCC pointed out that far from concentrating exclusively on Grenada, the regionwide survey had covered 22 separate Caribbean territories.

Democracy

One of the most important charges levelled against the PRG was that it frustrated the democratic process by refusing to hold parliamentary elections. This objection was dismissed by supporters of the revolution as irrelevant to the democratic development of Grenada which was based on popular participation on a day-to-day level rather than periodic elections. Moreover, they argued, the elections that had brought Gairy and, intermittently, Blaize to power were hardly models of democratic propriety. It is probably true that the NJM would have won any elections, since opposition in the form of the GULP and GNP was almost non-existent. But hostility to the 'Westminster model' was an ideological principle on the part of the NJM, and a constitutional commission was established to explore the institutionalisation of the revolution with an emphasis on 'continuous popular involvement'. Elections at an unspecified future date were expected to follow the commission's findings and a referendum. In the event, of course, the commission had barely begun its work when the invasion came.

The commission might well have recommended extending the process of decentralisation of power which had started in 1982. This involved the formation of six parish councils and 18 smaller zonal councils in a structure of local government and national consultation. At monthly meetings, these councils, open to all, debated local, national and international issues, including all important legislation. The most dramatic instances of popular participation took place when crowded public meetings throughout the island discussed the 1982 and 1983 budgets. The sense of political involvement felt by most Grenadians stood in stark contrast to the autocratic political system of 'parliamentary democracy' as practised by the previous regime.

Yet for all its innovations, the PRG's system of popular democracy had clear limitations. The conclusions of local councils were not binding upon the government which was, in essence, synonymous with the central committee of the NJM. Policy was therefore debated but not necessarily amended by popular participation. At the same time, the idea of accountability, while approved in principle, was never put into practice. Party appointments and structures remained unaffected by popular decision-making. Lastly, the system depended both on massive levels of participation and continual leadership from the NJM. Although half the population attended meetings for the first two years of the revolution, attendance gradually dropped. The NJM, with its exclusive, vanguardist membership policy, was also too small — in September 1983 it had a mere 65 full members — to organise the protracted popular mobilisation that was required. Inevitably, enthusiasm waned and the new democratic experiment lost its impetus.

In hindsight, the NJM made a tactical error in not moving more quickly towards elections which, most observers agree, would have confirmed its popularity. Political hostility from the US and its allies might have been reduced (although the experience of Nicaragua in 1984 has shown this not to be automatically the case), and the NJM would have had the opportunity to demonstrate fair and free elections to Grenadians more used to the traditional exercise in corruption and fraud. Nor would these elections have been incompatible with the local councils or the mass organisations. However, the authoritarian elements within the NJM were eventually to gain ascendancy within the tiny party, culminating in the events of October 1983. What might have evolved still further into genuine democracy and participation was ended by political elitism and militarism.

After the invasion, Grenada was nominally ruled by an appointed interim administration, but in fact controlled by the unelected Governor-General and US officials. The democratic contribution of ordinary Grenadians was minimal during the immediate post-invasion period; 'political activity' was effectively criminalised. When elections were considered politically safe and an appropriate party in the form of the NNP had been cobbled together, voting went ahead in a manner reminiscent of the Gairy era. With the success of the NNP, Grenada was judged by the US to have once again become a democracy.

Even though the term 'democracy' is open to wildly conflicting definitions, it cannot be claimed that the NNP government operated in a responsive or consultative manner. Dissident ministers resigned complaining of Prime Minister Blaize's autocratic style and alleging that the GNP faction within the government monopolised important posts. The opposition NDC pointed out that in the first 30 months of the NNP regime only 26 non-budget parliamentary meetings were convened. As a result, important legislation — the establishment of the ill-fated Grenada Airways and Discovery Television, the lease of Crown Lands in the GISCO fiasco — was passed without significant debate. Bills were pushed through all stages at one parliamentary sitting, thus reducing public debate on their contents. By the end of 1987, the NDC claimed, not one bill had been published for public comment and debate before its introduction in parliament.

The final collapse of the NNP government and the personal struggle between Blaize and Mitchell again exposed the former's disregard for parliamentary debate. As a vote of no confidence, supported both by the NDC and Mitchell's NNP threatened to force Blaize into dissolving parliament and calling general elections, the Prime Minister merely prorogued parliament, thereby postponing his downfall and keeping his minority faction in power. The NDC claimed that Blaize's constitutional manoeuvre reduced parliament to 'ridicule and contempt, making a mockery of parliamentary democracy'.

In addition, the recommendations of a constitutional review committee which were delivered to the government in November 1985 were simply shelved. The committee suggested removing the Prime Minister's right to appoint such key officials as the chief of police, the electoral commission chairman and public service commission members. It also recommended the appointment of an ombudsman, as well as calling for Grenada's return to the Eastern Caribbean judicial system. The government presumably saw such recommendations as politically inconvenient or unpalatable.

Equally, NNP promises to reintroduce local government, abolished by Gairy in 1968, came to nothing. These promises had raised hopes of democratic structures on a Village Council level, with special devolution of executive power to the ward islands of Carriacou and Petit Martinique. In September 1986, as it became obvious that inertia or fear of political defeat had stopped the process, Francis Alexis threatened to resign if elections were not held: 'as the minister responsible for local government, it is either we have local government elections or I damn quit.' By December, Alexis had resigned and the government never mentioned the issue again. The proposed reintroduction of local government featured in the NDC electoral campaign in March 1990, suggesting that Alexis's plans may yet materialise.

Whose Freedom?

According to the White House, Grenada is now a democracy, a free country in which human rights are respected and civil liberties guaranteed. In support of this claim, US officials point to a vigorous multi-party political system, competition between several weekly newspapers and a free-market economy that encourages foreign investment and individual enterprise. But such freedoms, while appreciated by those who traditionally hold political and economic power, contrast with the gradual loss of other freedoms and rights experienced by the majority of Grenadians. In particular, the abolition or downgrading of welfare reform programmes has removed automatic and free access to health and education, marking the return of a privileged private system for the wealthy minority. Alongside the reintroduction of institutionalised inequality stands the erosion of basic rights won by poor Grenadians during the PRG period: the right to work, the right to strike, the right to free health care and the right to education at all ages.

Although constitutionally elected, the NNP government did not hesitate to act undemocratically in the interests of 'national security'. Rights of free movement and assembly were curtailed, political censorship and expulsions became commonplace, parliamentary debate was kept to a minimum. Allegations of political victimisation, especially in the sweeping retrenchment scheme, abound, and are complemented by accusations of clientelism and corruption. In response to criticism, whether inside or outside Grenada, the NNP government appeared over-sensitive and vindictive. Beyond this, the government rests accused of presiding over a highly irregular political trial and of colluding with the US authorities in attempting the illegal extradition of a Grenadian national.

In its authoritarian actions and dislike of legitimate opposition the NNP government finally came close in certain respects to resembling its traditional political adversary, Eric Gairy, whose threatened return to power lay behind its creation. Not that a private militia has been used to terrorise opponents or that military personnel have been trained in Pinochet's Chile. But in legislation banning strikes, imposing states of emergency and restricting movement the parallels are evident.

Perhaps the greatest irony, however, surrounded a confidential internal party report that was leaked to the Caribbean News Agency (CANA) in November 1987. The report, drafted by a NNP special committee recommended a secret intelligence unit to carry out surveillance of other political organisations. It also suggested that NNP supporters should be placed in key civil service posts and that party MPs should be 'given the opportunity to participate in the selection and employment of party loyalists on government projects.' It is against this mixture of manipulation and cynicism that the rhetoric of liberation can be most accurately evaluated.

Chapter 5
Small Island, Big Issues

'In the not too distant future, I see businessmen flocking to the Caribbean. When they do, they will find a bounty of opportunity; they will find honest, hard-working people, happy and warm people, and they will find democratic government. That has to be a formula for good times ahead.'
Ronald Reagan, Grenada, 20 February 1986.

'The Americans arming these islands are making the same historical mistake the Grenadian revolutionaries made. The armies you set up to deter others always end up pointing their guns at the government and people. Who, I want to know, will guard the guards?'
James Mitchell, Prime Minister of St Vincent, July 1984.

Since the insurrection that toppled Gairy and established the PRG, Grenada has had a strategic and symbolic status out of all proportion to its tiny size and economic potential. It was the first English-speaking island in the Caribbean to undergo a revolutionary change of government. This stemmed from the unique phenomenon of Gairyism which went beyond other regional forms of personalism and corruption by also using political terrorism. For a period of 4½ years the island drew support from a wide range of governments, political organisations and individuals. By offering a practical alternative to the prevailing regional development model, the 'revo' won admirers as well as detractors from around the world.

Grenada then gained the sad distinction of being the first Commonwealth Caribbean territory to witness the political assassination of its leader. Six days later, it also became the first such territory to be invaded by US forces. Through these unprecedented events, the island assumed a global, if ephemeral, significance in the superpower context of the 1970s and 1980s. World opinion was overwhelmingly against the invasion; in the UN General Assembly vote of November 1983, 108 countries condemned the action as a violation of the UN Charter with only nine supporting the US position and 27 abstaining.

Grenada has also acquired a more lasting symbolic importance for the rest of the Caribbean, firstly as a model for economic and social reform within the framework of 'socialist orientation' and then as a blueprint for USAID-inspired restructuring and free-market deregulation. Its recent history has also had wider implications in terms of the region's growing militarisation and the related political development of neighbouring territories. Not least, Grenada's foreign policy has not only changed beyond recognition since the US invasion, but has also had an impact outside the Caribbean itself.

Foreign Policy

With the advent of formal independence since World War II, former colonies such as Grenada have been able to play an important role in world politics. As members of regional and world organisations — in Grenada's case, the Commonwealth, the Organisation of American States and the United Nations — their votes count and are judged as indicators of their superpower allegiance or non-aligned position. For Grenada, this symbolic demonstration of ideological commitment has moved from a strongly anti-US foreign policy position to one which has been condemned as slavishly pro-Washington.

During the PRG years, Grenada was anxious to court economic aid from such Third World sources as Libya, Iraq, Algeria and Syria by adopting a high-profile series of 'principled positions' in its foreign policy. These included siding with the Soviet Union over the invasion of Afghanistan (despite serious reservations from some NJM central committee members and Cuba), support for the Palestine Liberation Organisation and the African National Congress and continual attacks on 'imperialism' and 'Zionism'. Extravagant gestures such as offering to send 500 Grenadian troops to fight in Namibia were accompanied by pragmatic bridge-building with the European Economic Community and the social-democratic Socialist International. Aid from the Soviet bloc, economic and military, was forthcoming alongside that from a varied range of sources, but the Soviet Union remained cautious in its political and military dealings with Grenada.

Revolutionary Grenada's principal ally, however, was Cuba, relieved to find a friendly left-wing state in a predominantly hostile

Caribbean. Financial and technical assistance from the larger island was extremely generous — the Cuban contribution towards the airport alone was valued at US$60 million — and in return, the PRG adopted Havana's line on foreign policy. Grenada used the Non-Aligned Movement, in particular, as an arena for anti-US rhetoric, while establishing links with pro-Cuban political parties throughout the Caribbean. It was primarily this open alliance with Cuba — for years Washington's national security obsession — that soured relations between Grenada and the US.

With the invasion, Grenada did an about face. Links with radical Third World regimes and the Soviet bloc were cut or allowed to wither away. Cuban equipment at the airport was simply confiscated, and debts to eastern bloc countries were left unpaid on the advice of USAID officials. Instead, Grenada established diplomatic and commercial ties with right-wing countries such as South Korea and Taiwan. With Japan's rising influence in the region, Grenada has been courting that country's aid as have all the other dependent Caribbean economies. But the most remarkable transformation has been in Grenada's shift from intransigent 'anti-imperialism' to a 'special relationship' with the US. In the United Nations Grenada's 71.3 per cent pro-US voting rate between 1984 and 1986 was the highest of any Third World country.

Having supported the US on the 'Star Wars' issue, withdrawal from UNESCO, sanctions against Nicaragua and aid to the Contras, Grenada finally went to extraordinary lengths to display its loyalty in 1985 and 1986 by voting against sanctions against South Africa. In 1985, of the 18 countries voting against sanctions (122 voted for), Grenada was the only Third World country and the only country with a black population. In voting against, Grenada sided with the US, Britain, Israel and the other NATO states. The response in the island and among Grenadians in the US was one of widespread disbelief and shame. Subsequent government statements on the issue spoke somewhat unconvincingly of a 'misunderstanding', and ministers tried to repair the island's image by rhetorical attacks on apartheid. Such excuses could not dispel the commonly held view that the Grenadian government was simply an uncritical accomplice of US foreign policy. The view was to some extent reinforced in the spring of 1986 when Grenada sided with the US over the bombing of its former ally Libya from British military bases.

The Caribbean Right
The Grenadian revolution posed the threat to the US State Department

of spreading radicalisation throughout the Caribbean Basin. Along
with Cuba and Nicaragua, the island seemed to embody the
time-honoured domino theory which foresaw the spreading of
'communism' from one poor Third World country to another. In
reality, a certain process of radicalisation did occur in other Caribbean
territories. Left-wing parties in nearby St Lucia and St Vincent made
considerable gains in support and influence, while Dominica had a
short-lived interim government containing two radical ministers. In
late 1979, the PRG issued a 'Declaration of St George's' in association
with representatives of the Dominica Labour Party and the St Lucia
Labour Party. The statement of common principles and positions was
followed by a demonstration which featured the slogan 'St Vincent
next!' The PRG's first year of power also coincided with the final
months of Michael Manley's reformist government in Jamaica, with
both governments sharing a penchant for anti-US policy statements.
Other perceived anti-US regimes were those in Guyana, where the
authoritarian personalism and mismanagement of the Forbes Burnham
regime masqueraded as 'cooperative socialism', and Surinam, where
a self-defined progressive military junta had seized power in February
1980. In Washington, this looked like a dangerous left-wing tide.

Jim Rudin

Maurice Bishop (second right) chairs meeting between left-wing leaderships
of Grenada, St Lucia and Dominica, 1979. Bernard Coard is first on left

The invasion was greeted by US strategists as a crucial turning point in the regional advance of the left. In fact, that advance had already been halted partly through the left's own sectarianism and electoral incompetence. As a result, conservative parties in the Caribbean won a series of electoral contests that left Grenada as the exception rather than the rule. The reverse was also partly a consequence of a programme of US destabilisation which culminated in 1980, when Michael Manley lost power to the right-wing JLP led by Edward Seaga. Already in December 1979, the conservative St Vincent Labour Party had won a sweeping victory against the left even though it was unusually unified and confident in its electoral campaign. In Dominica, the robustly pro-US Freedom Party, led by Eugenia Charles, routed the left in July 1980, while in May 1982 John Compton and his United Workers Party won another right-wing victory in St Lucia. In Antigua, meanwhile, the left-wing and pro-NJM Antigua Caribbean Liberation Movement received only four per cent of the vote in the April 1980 election (this had sunk to two per cent by early 1989).

In electoral terms, the Caribbean left had not made the breakthrough that the US feared. Conservative regimes of a highly traditional type were installed in almost all English-speaking Caribbean countries by 1983, and this made it possible for the US to gain the support of a majority of regional governments for its invasion plans. The events of October 1983 therefore merely confirmed a right-wing trend in the Caribbean, further fracturing an already divided left into sectarian disputes which continue to the present day. While a small minority of political parties continued to support the NJM, as represented by the imprisoned central committee members, others, led by the Cuban government, endorsed the position of the MBPM. Right-wing parties took advantage of the malaise which seemed to affect all radical groups and politicians in the region. Seaga called a snap election in Jamaica only two months after the invasion and two full years before his term of office was due to expire. Buoyed up by his direct, if secondary, role in supporting the US action and a general mood of anti-communism, Seaga's JLP was returned for a further five years in an election boycotted by Manley's PNP.

The events immediately preceding the invasion had also created widespread revulsion throughout the Caribbean. Maurice Bishop had been a popular and respected figure in the region, even among some of the neighbouring territories' more conservative political leaders. The fact that he and a significant number of innocent civilians had been murdered in what amounted to a military coup caused deep shock within the English-speaking Caribbean, which has little experience of political assassinations. It also provided the regional forces of conservatism with an unprecedented propaganda weapon. They could claim that all revolutions were liable to end in sectarian bloodshed and that 'Marxism', as personified by the RMC and the 'Coard faction' of the NJM, was synonymous with violence and militarism.

Right-wing dominance in the Caribbean grew in the years following the invasion. The groups and parties of the left that had come to prominence at the same time as the NJM became increasingly marginalised and introverted. Meanwhile, regional conservatives formed the Caribbean Democratic Union (CDU) in 1986 as an arm of the worldwide International Democratic Union, founded by Ronald Reagan and Margaret Thatcher. Including the then ruling parties of Jamaica, Dominica, Montserrat, Belize, St Kitts-Nevis, St Lucia, St Vincent and Grenada, the CDU enthusiastically supported US political and economic objectives for the region. In return, US funding was channelled to the organisation from the Republican Party and the National Endowment for Democracy (NED), a conservative US body funded by federal grants and linked to USAID and AIFLD. The powerful CDU easily dominated a largely inactive Caribbean Community and Common Market (CARICOM), successfully pressing for pro-US positions on such regional issues as Haiti and Cuba. It also built on advances in regional right-wing cooperation, as seen in the Grenada elections of 1984, when Seaga's JLP contributed substantially to the NNP campaign.

The electoral victory of Michael Manley in February 1989 was seen by some as a turning regional tide. Although clearly a setback to the JLP and Seaga as undisputed leader of the CDU, the return to power of a much chastened and avowedly moderate Manley could not be judged as heralding a Caribbean-wide shift to the left. Indeed, so moderate was Manley's early political programme that Eugenia Charles of Dominica was perhaps half-serious when she asked whether he intended to join the CDU. Yet however much Manley seeks to dissociate himself from the radicalism of the 1970s, his victory shows that Caribbean electorates can become disenchanted with the free-market policies of an Edward Seaga. So far, however, this has not become a region-wide trend. Electoral victories in 1989 by conservative parties in Antigua, St Kitts-Nevis and St Vincent all confirmed the rightward shift in evidence since the early 1980s and strengthened by events in Grenada.

Colonialism and Militarisation

The crisis of October 1983 also confirmed two other trends within the region. Firstly, it completed the replacement of Britain by the US as the pre-eminent political power in the Commonwealth Caribbean. The official version of events suggests that London was not consulted on the invasion plans, since US military planners feared that a joint operation would be a disaster. It is firmly believed elsewhere, however, that the British government did know of the imminent invasion but chose to feign ignorance, thereby minimising the awkward implications of the situation by presenting the Commonwealth and British public with what looked like a *fait accompli*. Its apparent inaction in regard to the coup and subsequent political events was thus widely viewed as either lethargy or indifference, but this was perhaps the price that had to be paid for avoiding politically costly direct involvement in the invasion. As it was, the Thatcher government found itself saddled with an embarrassing constitutional situation *vis-a-vis* the Governor-General and the Queen (see p.42) and chose to express muted and short-lived disapproval of the invasion.

The implications of Britain's apparent irrelevance were not lost on regional politicians who wished to display their approval of the US action. Seaga, capitalising on his affinity with the Reagan administration, claimed that the English-speaking Caribbean countries felt 'a certain amount of bitterness' over London's response to Grenada. Britain, he concluded, could no longer expect 'some right of prior consultation in matters that affect us here.' For Tom Adams, an equally vehement supporter of the US military action, the invasion was of historic significance: 'In hemispheric terms, 1983 is bound to be seen as the watershed year in which the influence of the United States, willy-nilly, came observably to replace that of Great Britain in the old British colonies.' To many, Britain's marginal role in the Grenada crisis only served to reinforce the impression that the former colonial power was an increasingly irrelevant force in the region. The extended economic crisis of 1979-83, the introduction of the anti-immigration Nationality Bill (1981) and a general relinquishment of regional responsibilities had all given the impression that Britain was an increasingly insular and unimportant country.

Subsequent policy statements from the British Foreign Office have tried to give a dynamic profile to London's attitude towards the Caribbean, and a number of ministers have visited the region and made speeches emphasising Britain's special links with the Commonwealth territories. In reality, however, British policy has largely complemented Washington's programme of economic and political goals. British aid has been targetted at Caribbean police forces, since the 1974 congressional Foreign Assistance Act forbids the training of foreign police by the US. The US, meanwhile, has concentrated on arming and training the para-military SSUs, which, for the sake of Congress, are defined as 'militias' rather than 'police'. Overall, British political presence and prestige in the Caribbean have continued to dwindle steadily, as the sums of aid dispensed remain insignificant in relation even to falling US assistance to the region. A few important British companies remain active in the Eastern Caribbean, notably Geest plc and Cable & Wireless, while Britain's diplomatic presence is limited and low-key. Britain does, however, remain important as a trading partner, buying some 35 per cent of Grenadian exports and providing about 30 per cent of its imports.

Britain's decline and the supremacy of the US were perhaps best illustrated by the respective post-invasion visits to Grenada by the Queen and President Reagan. The Queen's visit in October 1986 was greeted by widespread apathy and low turnouts at her public appearances. Reagan's 4½-hour visit, however, drew a 15,000-strong

President Reagan's visit, February 1986

crowd to Queen's Park, and most there greeted his brief speech enthusiastically. Not, however, that the US Embassy had taken any risks. Posters all around the island advertised the event, promising free refreshments and other inducements. What emerged from the visit in concrete terms for Grenada was disappointing: in a series of regional grants and concessions Reagan promised 1,500 scholarships for Caribbean students over three years, an extension of the CBI programme to Caribbean-produced textiles and a US$5.5 million grant to the regional judiciary.

The second trend consolidated by October 1983 was the region's growing militarisation. This, too, predated the invasion itself, and can be traced back to the sense of vulnerability felt by regional governments in the preceding four years. The effortless overthrow of Gairy in March 1979 by some 40 NJM insurgents was the first event to worry other leaders in the Eastern Caribbean. It was followed by a series of unsuccessful coup attempts against Eugenia Charles in Dominica in 1981, two of which were led by members of the Dominica Defence Force. The Defence Force was eventually disbanded and constitutional rule restored, but not before French troops from neighbouring Martinique had intervened to stop the rebellion. A smaller uprising involving a handful of armed Rastafarians on the St Vincent dependency of Union Island had also taken place in December 1979. On this occasion, police from Barbados had been flown in to help the St Vincent government regain control.

In October 1982, the Prime Ministers of Antigua, Barbados, Dominica, St Lucia and St Vincent signed a 'Memorandum of Understanding' which formalised cooperation in matters of individual and collective security. The agreement foresaw an eventual regional force of 1,000 troops and police, with an administrative centre in Barbados. This was the beginning of the Regional Security System (RSS). Although largely concerned with countering smuggling and possible mercenary attack (Dominica had been the target for a bizarre Ku Klux Klan mercenary coup attempt in 1981), the Memorandum contained other obvious implications. As Prime Minister Vere Bird of Antigua put it:

> The whole idea behind the Defence Force is that if so called revolutionaries get through today on your own island, don't forget there will be forces in all the other islands and you will have to answer for them. In this region, we cannot afford another Cuba or another Grenada. If this was ever to happen, our people will never be able to live in peace.

Such views naturally coincided with US perceptions of Grenada. A small US security team moved into the Embassy in Barbados, and military personnel were installed in Antigua. By February 1983, 30 US military advisors were stationed in the Eastern Caribbean.

The invasion, with its token contribution from Caribbean governments, was to be retroactively justified by reference to the 1981 Charter of the Organisation of Eastern Caribbean States. In reality, however, it was the 'Memorandum of Understanding' of 1982 which provided the framework for the cosmetic involvement of 350 paramilitary personnel from Antigua, Barbados, Dominica, Jamaica, St Lucia and St Vincent. But the invasion also marked an escalation in regional militarisation which was far from cosmetic. As well as sending military trainers to Grenada itself, the US dispatched teams of eight army staff to five small Eastern Caribbean islands and larger teams to Barbados and Jamaica. These Green Beret teams led six-week SSU training cycles with police cadets on their home islands, and the trained personnel then went on to constitute permanent 40 to 80-member SSUs in each island. Each graduated unit also spent a period within the Caribbean Peacekeeping Force in Grenada until it was disbanded in 1985.

The US investment in the SSUs was considerable. From a figure of US$1.2 million in 1982, US military aid to the Eastern Caribbean rose to US$7.2 million in 1984 and US$8.5 million in 1985, figures which included three coastguard vessels valued at US$1.4 million each. In addition, the training and equipment for the CPF on Grenada cost US$15 million. This influx of US military aid brought an unprecedented array of hardware into the region: M-16 rifles and submachine guns, rocket and grenade launchers, telecommunications and radio systems, uniforms and armoured vehicles. Even so, the total expenditure was much lower than that envisaged by Tom Adams in the immediate aftermath of the Grenada invasion. When George Shultz visited Barbados and Grenada in February 1984, for instance, Adams reportedly presented him with a plan for an 1,800 strong standing army with headquarters in Bridgetown. The cost was estimated at US$100 million. The US, however, was not enthusiastic about a 'Caribbean NATO', especially at such cost. The idea has subsequently faded away, leaving the individual SSUs under the umbrella of the more modest Regional Security System.

Complementing the domestic SSUs has been an increase in visible US military might in the region. Annual military manoeuvres such as 'Exotic Palm' in 1985 and 'Ocean Venture' in 1986 involved thousands of US troops, but also significant numbers of Caribbean personnel. The 1986 exercise, for instance, featured an imaginary invasion of Grenada and mobilised 1,000 troops and police from the US, Jamaica, Antigua,

Philip Wolmuth

Caribbean Peacekeeping Force on patrol in St George's

Dominica, Grenada, St Kitts-Nevis and St Lucia. It is widely believed that the manoeuvre was timed to coincide with the opening of the Maurice Bishop murder trial in St George's. Such coincidences are not uncommon; in March 1989, on the tenth anniversary of the insurrection that installed the PRG, the MBPM held a commemorative conference and rally. Not only were Grenada's police unusually active in stopping and searching cars for the duration of the conference, but the USS *Harlan County* appeared in St George's port on the day of the anniversary, ostensibly for its crew to play a local team at basketball.

The militarisation process, however, has had influential critics. Prime Minister James Mitchell of St Vincent has publicly condemned the Regional Security System as a waste of resources and up until 1990 forbade Vincentian personnel to take part in regional manoeuvres. Following the death of the conservative Tom Adams, a strong supporter of US regional policy, the Barbados Democratic Labour Party under the leadership of Errol Barrow was returned to power. Barrow was a long-standing champion of Caribbean sovereignty and was sceptical of US regional concerns and the military build-up. He restricted Barbadian involvement in the RSS to a minimum and accused Eugenia Charles and John Compton of 'getting President Reagan to play Santa Claus'. Since Barrow's death in June 1987 the Barbadian government has continued his policies. Moreover, Trinidad and Tobago — the Eastern Caribbean's major economic power — has consistently refused to become part of any regional military bloc. Having opposed the invasion itself, Trinidad stands as an obstacle to further militarisation.

The case of Grenada demonstrates that in practice the SSU is much less a regional defence unit (most Caribbean governments tacitly accept that regional defence is the prerogative of the US) than a vehicle for internal security concerns. The NNP government used SSU personnel against anti-US demonstrators at the time of the Reagan visit. It also sent a fully equipped SSU unit to arrest the operator of a private radio station and to close down the premises in July 1985. When death sentences were imposed on the defendants in the Maurice Bishop murder trial, Prime Minister Blaize invoked the terms of the Regional Security System and demanded reinforcements from neighbouring territories. On the basis of such politically motivated actions, the SSUs are viewed with understandable misgivings by many in Grenada who have clear memories of a brief and unloved military regime in October 1983.

Failure of a Model

Whether caused by left-wing sectarianism, inability to deal with the electoral system, or, as some claim, the region's innate conservatism, radical politics in the English-speaking Caribbean have not found their way into the mainstream. The 'new' Manley, the abandonment of 'socialist' rhetoric in post-Forbes Burnham Guyana and the continuing marginalisation of radical parties in the Eastern Caribbean are all symptoms of a regional, and global, retreat from left-wing ideology. Given the lack of left-wing alternatives, the regional right has effectively had free rein to impose its version of development on the Caribbean. The active intervention of the US in every sphere of the region's political and social life — through aid programmes, business investment, the media, evangelism and military presence — has supported the right's hegemony. It has also allowed the US view of the Caribbean's economic and strategic role to prevail.

The current US prescription for the Caribbean revolves around the opening up of regional economies to foreign investment and the creation of employment through the development of the so-called Free Trade Zones (FTZs). In early 1990, there were perhaps 50 such FTZs, mainly in Jamaica and the Dominican Republic, generating at most 200,000 jobs. Their appeal to US capital comes from a package of tax exemptions, no restrictions on profit repatriation, a trade union-free environment, low wages and a 'disciplined female labour force'. The companies investing in the Caribbean are involved not only in assembly and manufacturing, but increasingly in data processing, facilitated by improved communications between the islands and the US.

Tourism is the other main factor in the US-approved development strategy for the Caribbean. Countries such as the Dominican Republic have hugely increased their tourist industry in the course of the 1980s, and in some islands — St Lucia, Barbados, Antigua — tourism is probably the principal economic activity and source of employment. In contrast, agriculture has declined in importance throughout the Caribbean, due partly to changing consumer tastes in the North (entailing reduced demand for sugar, tobacco, coffee and cocoa), partly to a generalised rural-urban drift and partly to declining domestic production and increased food imports.

The shift towards tourism and service industries has done nothing to improve the economic crisis which hit the Caribbean most severely in the 1970s with raised oil import prices and declining terms of trade for exports. As a result, debt servicing has risen dramatically. As a percentage of export earnings, Jamaica's debt servicing stood at 40 per cent in 1990 as opposed to 19.3 per cent in 1980, while Grenada's had risen from 4.1 per cent in 1980 to 20.3 per cent in 1987. Unemployment, too, is a region-wide problem, ranging from around 25 per cent or more in most English-speaking territories (possibly as high as 40 per cent in Jamaica and Guyana) to an estimated 70 per cent in Haiti. Economic suffering of this sort has produced inevitable survival strategies — the growth of informal and illegal economic activity (street-vending, domestic work, black marketeering, the drug trade), massive migration within and from the region, dependence on hard currency remittances from relatives abroad. Meanwhile, state provision in health, education and housing has been reduced in every territory and in some is almost non-existent.

The present US-endorsed economic model has had little impact on the mounting Caribbean crisis, and indeed has probably contributed to it. Low wages, tax breaks and repatriated profits mean that the FTZs reinforce poverty and contribute little to Caribbean economies; only 35 per cent of foreign exchange generated, it is estimated, remains in the countries in question. The nature of enclave tourism, too, results in limited earnings for Caribbean countries and high profits for foreign airlines and hotel multinationals. Often no linkages between tourism and the rest of the economy exist, and money spent by tourists is offset by imports of food and other materials for the industry.

The CBI aid, trade and investment package, in particular, has been an acknowledged failure. Not only did some Caribbean products already enjoy low duty concessions, but others such as textiles were initially excluded under the terms of the programme. CBI has encouraged the growth of an export-led agricultural sector, sending 'winter vegetables' like tomatoes, water melons and pineapples to the US, but this economic stimulus has effectively been wiped out by US reductions in the Caribbean's quotas for sugar exports. What Washington has given with one hand it has taken away with the other.

'Official' development strategies in the Caribbean seem increasingly discredited at the beginning of the 1990s. Grenada is no exception in this respect, even if high rates of growth have been achieved for several years through favourable exchange rates, aid-generated construction and tourism. Despite this, unemployment remains unacceptably high, incomes low and public services chronically run down. Worse, the US plan to establish a viable manufacturing sector has clearly failed, and foreign capital — unlike in Jamaica or the Dominican Republic — has simply refused to appear. President Reagan's vision of 'businessmen flocking to the Caribbean' thus seems more and more like a mirage in Grenada. While the island's politicians prefer to blame one another for mismanagement and corruption, what seems more evident is that the development model itself does not work.

The failure of the model is all the more telling in Grenada, given the symbolic importance attached to the island by the invasion. Here was an opportunity to demonstrate the economic benefits of export-led, private-sector development, to set an example for the rest of the Caribbean. With large amounts of bilateral aid, the prospect of CBI, promises of investment and the personal commitment of President Reagan himself, the future for Grenada seemed exceptionally bright. And yet because almost nothing actually materialised, the island relies once more on its traditional agricultural exports and upon the precarious business of attracting tourists.

The dismal experience of post-invasion Grenada reveals much about the limitations of a certain notion of development. It also casts new light on the short-lived experiment of the PRG and its results. For all its failings — and few would deny that there were major shortcomings — the revolution at least offered hope and an alternative to the poor of the Caribbean and beyond. Its uniqueness lay in offering such an alternative within the constraints of a dependent and under-developed micro-state. As a result, it succeeded in promoting a broader debate about the real possibilities of development in an under-developed part of the world. That debate, at least, continues.

Conclusion
'A One-Night Stand'

'There was a sort of Marshall Plan mentality. We just dumped in lots of money and lots of investors and suddenly they would all mix up and we would be back on this tremendous growth path. But development is never that way. Grenada has to come to grips with the reality of development'.
James Holtaway, USAID Regional Director, May 1989.

During the 1988 US presidential election campaign, Vice-President-to-be Dan Quayle hailed Grenada as one of the outgoing Reagan administration's major foreign policy successes. Although this view was relatively commonplace for a year or more after the invasion, it has become increasingly rare. Instead, Grenada, with its once powerful symbolic message of resurgent US might and militant anti-communism, has faded into obscurity. This is partly due to new political attitudes, generated by changing East-West relations and a reduction in Cold War tensions. The Bush administration currently does not see the Caribbean as an important security threat, and President Gorbachev has made it clear that the USSR does not wish to support revolutionary movements in the western hemisphere. But the silence surrounding Grenada is also due to the embarrassing failure of the development project which the US imposed on the island and its allies in government tried to administer. Failure, ultimately, does not make good propaganda, and there is little to celebrate in Grenada.

What has the US achieved since October 1983? Large capital grants have repaired war damage, upgraded aspects of the island's infrastructure and laid the basis for a manufacturing sector aimed at foreign investors. Politically, a pro-US government somehow survived five years in power and oversaw the widescale reversal of the PRG's policies and programme. The perceived threats of Eric Gairy and the left were more or less contained during this period, even if in the 1990 elections Gairy narrowly failed to return to power. The private sector has been restored to its traditional place in the island, while a handful of foreign investors has sought to take advantage of a generous set of incentives and tax-breaks. Due to high world prices for agricultural exports, favourable exchange rates and an increase in tourism, the island's economy has grown, while remaining highly undiversified and vulnerable.

These, however, are modest achievements when compared to the high expectations encouraged among Grenadians after the invasion. In contrast to the innovative blend of social reformism and economic diversification advocated by the PRG, they are also strikingly unoriginal in their aims. The general thrust of post-invasion policy has been to return the island to its pre-revolutionary status quo, while adding expanded tourism and offshore manufacturing to its limited economic repertoire. Certain elements of the PRG programme have been maintained, but names have been changed and budgets cut in a profound shift of priorities.

More disturbing is the price paid by most Grenadians for an unsuccessful experiment in economic deregulation. Education, health

Pro-US graffiti in Tempe, St George's

Philip Wolmuth

and housing have all deteriorated dramatically, while the burden of
indirect taxation has fallen disproportionately on those least able to
pay. Per capita income has barely kept pace with inflation, and public
sector cuts have massively increased unemployment. The NNP
government, despite its optimistic forecasts, persistently teetered on
the brink of bankruptcy, unable to collect the taxes it imposed on the
advice of its US backers. At the same time, freedoms and rights — the
ostensible basis for the invasion itself — have been selectively defined
and applied, especially as regards radical groups and individuals who
challenge the new orthodoxy.

At the root of this failure has been the inability of government and
the US to attract foreign capital to Grenada, thereby creating jobs and
services to replace the demolished public sector. This, together with
gradually declining levels of US aid, has fuelled disillusionment and
resentment against the US. Far from being the island's 'saviour', the
US is now more and more seen as a purveyor of broken promises.
This feeling was well encapsulated in an article by US writer Gary
Krist in an April 1989 edition of the conservative journal, *The New
Republic*:

> To put it mildly, our presence here — particularly in the poorer
> western and northwestern sections of the island — no longer
> occasions the universal adoration that is supposed to be our due
> as heroic champions of democracy... The reason for our cool
> reception is not entirely clear, but it seems to have less to do with
> our invasion/imperialist rescue/adventure mission itself than
> with the follow-up. That vast flood of American investment in
> Grenada, much anticipated in the years following the invasion,
> has not materialized. Although the Agency for International
> Development has helped build some dandy roads and a nice
> mental hospital on a hill below Fort George (presumably to
> replace the one we accidentally bombed), US companies have
> overwhelmingly decided that wonderful opportunities lie
> elsewhere. And now that Uncle Sam is starting to cut back on the
> economic aid (to a still hefty $10 million a year, after pumping
> $110 million into the country over five years), people are getting
> the impression that Grenada, having served its public relations
> function, will now be cast aside like a jilted lover. And to be
> honest, who can blame them? What started out as a marriage
> made in heaven has begun to look more like a one-night stand.

Disenchantment with US development plans has been paralleled by
disillusionment with the political process itself. Where during the PRG
period there was intense mobilisation and politicisation, there is now

apathy and cynicism. The young, especially, see themselves as disenfranchised and are turning in increasing numbers towards emigration. The main political parties do not inspire enthusiasm or confidence among most Grenadians, as demonstrated by the low turn out in the elections of March 1990.

The NDC government, unstable from the outset, will inherit these major problems. Yet, beyond US indifference and local disenchantment, there is another obstacle that Grenada's rulers will have to face for many years. The revolutionary period, while creating its own problems and failures, nevertheless gave most Grenadians a memorable taste of independence and participation. Despite the trauma and apathy that followed, the memory has endured and for many is bound up with the person of Maurice Bishop. That the NNP government should have commemorated the anniversary of Bishop's murder is indicative of popular respect for the former Prime Minister.

Whether nostalgia for Bishop's charismatic leadership is likely to be translated into support for a new revolutionary programme is altogether more debatable. But Bishop's legacy and the experience of the PRG years remain a powerful force in Grenada and are not underestimated by the more perceptive younger generation of

Mark Wilson

Memorial to Maurice Bishop in St George's cemetery

politicians such as Keith Mitchell and George Brizan. The brief experiment in self-determination and economic independence has left a lasting mark in other ways. A tradition of small-scale cooperative venture has survived the US-inspired crusade for privatisation and owes much to innovations from the revolutionary period. National and international agencies are continuing this tradition, assisting groups and communities in agricultural and manufacturing cooperatives. At the same time, the popularity of the USAID-funded 'Special Development Activities' programme reveals the enduring influence of the community self-help schemes initiated by the PRG. As programmes and projects started by the PRG now begin to bear fruit — the airport, the cocoa rehabilitation scheme, the health centres, etc — so the dynamism of that period stands in greater contrast to the inertia of the post-invasion regimes.

The failure of US policy in Grenada has not been spectacular in economic terms, although it is clear that extensive financial assistance has not created the sought-after investment and prosperity. Grenada is no poorer than its small Eastern Caribbean neighbours, yet nor is it any richer despite exceptional inflows of US money, amounting to US$1,100 for every Grenadian. The failure has rather been in the inability of US technocrats and Grenadian politicians to create an alternative to the PRG's blend of reform and state-led development which actually enjoys real popular support. Instead of discrediting the PRG experiment by achieving the healthy free-market democracy envisaged by USAID, the post-invasion regime and its US supporters have discarded imaginative policies in favour of an unworkable orthodoxy. The final irony of post-invasion Grenada is that despite great promises and high expectations, the island has merely returned to the economic stagnation and political disenchantment which led to revolution in the first place.

Further Reading

Mark Adkin, *Urgent Fury: The Battle for Grenada*. Leo Cooper, London, 1989.

Fitzroy Ambursley and James Dunkerley, *Grenada: Whose Freedom?* Latin America Bureau, London, 1984.

Tom Barry, Beth Wood and Deb Preusch, *The Other Side of Paradise: Foreign Control in the Caribbean*. Grove Press, New York, 1984.

George Brizan, *Grenada: Island of Conflict*. Zed Books, London, 1984.

Jan Carew, *Grenada: The Hour Will Strike Again*. International Organisation of Journalists, Prague, 1985.

Steve Clark, 'The Second Assassination of Maurice Bishop' in *New International*, New York, no 6, 1987.

Bernard Coard, *Village and Workers, Women, Farmers and Youth Assemblies During the Grenada Revolution: Their Genesis, Evolution and Significance*. Caribbean Labour Solidarity/NJM/Karia Press, London, 1989.

Phyllis Coard, *US War on One Woman: My Conditions of Imprisonment in Grenada*. Karia Press, London, 1988.

Leon Cornwall, *The Grenada 'Elections': An Analysis from Behind Prison Bars*. Caribbean Labour Solidarity, London, 1985.

Grenada: Report of a Labour Movement Delegation, December 1983. London, 1984.

Grenada: The Peaceful Revolution. EPICA, Washington DC, 1983.

Gordon K. Lewis, *Grenada: The Jewel Despoiled*. Johns Hopkins University Press, Baltimore, 1987.

In Nobody's Backyard: Maurice Bishop's Speeches, 1979-1983. Edited by Chris Searle. Zed Books, London, 1984.

Kathy McAfee, 'Hurricane: IMF, World Bank, U.S.AID in the Caribbean'. *NACLA Report on the Americas*, Washington DC, February 1990.

Manning Marable, *African and Caribbean Politics: From Kwame Nkrumah to Maurice Bishop*. Verso, London, 1987.

NACLA Report on the Americas, 'Mare Nostrum: US Security Policy in the English-speaking Caribbean'. Washington DC, July/August 1985.

Hugh O'Shaughnessy, *Grenada: Revolution, Invasion and Aftermath*.

Sphere Books, London, 1984

Anthony Payne, Paul Sutton and Tony Thorndike, *Grenada: Revolution and Invasion*. London, Croom Helm, 1984.

Jenny Pearce, *Under the Eagle: US Intervention in Central America and the Caribbean*. Latin America Bureau, London, 1982.

Gregory Sandford and Richard Vigilante, *Grenada: The Untold Story*. Madison, New York, 1984.

Chris Searle, *Grenada Morning: A Memoir of the 'Revo'*. Karia Press, London, 1989.

Chris Searle, *Grenada: The Struggle Against Destabilization*. Writers and Readers, London, 1983.

A.W. Singham, *The Hero and the Crowd in a Colonial Polity*. Yale University Press, New Haven, 1968.

Catherine Sunshine, *The Caribbean: Survival, Struggle and Sovereignty*. EPICA, Washington DC, 1985 (updated edition, 1988).

Robert Thompson, 'Towards Agricultural Self-Reliance in Grenada: An Alternative Model', in P.I. Gomes (ed.), *Rural Development in the Caribbean*. Heinemann, Kingston, Jamaica, 1985.

Tony Thorndike, *Grenada: Politics, Economics and Society*. Frances Pinter, London, 1985.

Tony Thorndike, 'Militarisation in the Commonwealth Caribbean', in Peter Calvert (ed), *The Central American Security System*. Cambridge University Press, Cambridge, 1988.

Vijay Tiwathia, *The Grenada War: Anatomy of a Low-Intensity Conflict*. Lancer International, New Delhi, 1987.

Bob Woodward, *Veil: The Secret Wars of the CIA 1981-1987*. Simon and Schuster, New York, 1987.

Reliable and up-to-date information on Grenada and the rest of the Caribbean region can be found in two monthly publications:

Caribbean Contact, PO Box 616, Bridgetown, Barbados.

Caribbean Insight, Commonwealth House, 18 Northumberland Avenue, London WC2N 5RA.

Index

LAB books on the Caribbean include:

Far From Paradise: An Introduction to Caribbean Development
James Ferguson

Traces Caribbean history from Columbus to the present day, looking at slavery, the colonial period,the struggle for independence and the rise of US regional influence. Large format, highly illustrated.

64 pages   £4.99/US$7.95   ISBN 0 906156 54 8   1990

Cuba: The Test of Time
Jean Stubbs

'A lively and searching analysis of Cuba by a writer who knows the country intimately.' Hugh O'Shaughnessy, *Observer* Latin America Correspondent

142 pages   £5.75/US$9.50   ISBN 0 906156 42 4   1989

The Poor and the Powerless: Economic Policy and Change in the Caribbean
Clive Y Thomas

'A historical and contemporary survey of Caribbean economic development armed with a degree of detail which makes it, at the most fundamental level, a useful reference work as well as a good introduction to the region.'
Caribbean Insight

396 pages   £11.00/US$13.50   ISBN 0 906156 35 1   1988

Green Gold: Bananas and Dependency in the Eastern Caribbean
Robert Thomson

'In slightly less than 100 pages, Robert Thomson has told one of the most interesting stories about small island economies that any reader is likely to peruse in a lifetime. This volume is a must for any Caribbean scholar.'
Times of the Americas

96 pages   £5.25/US$9.00   ISBN 0 906156 26 2   1987

Prices are for paperback editions and include post and packing. For a complete list of books write to the Latin America Bureau, 1 Amwell Street, London EC1R 1UL. LAB books are distributed in North America by Monthly Review Press, 122 West 27th Street, New York NY10001